Betty's Wartime Diary

1939-1945

Edited by Nicholas Webley

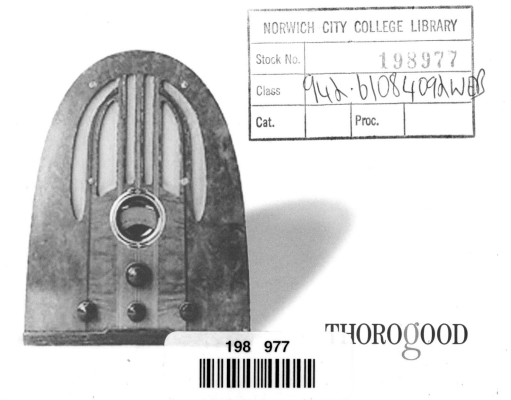

THOROGOOD

Reprinted July 2003 by Thorogood
10-12 Rivington Street
London EC2A 3DU
Telephone: 020 7749 4748 • Fax: 020 7729 6110
Email: info@thorogood.ws • Web: www.thorogood.ws

A CIP catalogue record for this book is available
from the British Library.

ISBN 1 85418 221 8

Printed in India by Replika Press Pvt. Ltd.

Designed by Driftdesign

ACKNOWLEDGEMENTS

Thanks to the family of Clyde G. Whitt for their kind assistance; The National Archives and Records Administration, Library of Congress; The Ministry of Defence; J. D. Ross for their assistance in locating various posters (http://www.openstore.com/posters/index.html); Tim, without whose help this would have taken much longer; Pat Hall for her encouragement; all at Thorogood; Sir Malcolm Bradbury for being so generous with his advice; Douglas Adams for being such an inspiration and who is much missed; Barry at Cawtec Computers for building my PC and keeping it up to the job in hand.

COPYRIGHT DISCLAIMER

MAP OF EAST ANGLIA

Listed on the map below are some of the places mentioned by Betty in her diary, including the airbases of Swanton Morley, Coltishall and Wendling.

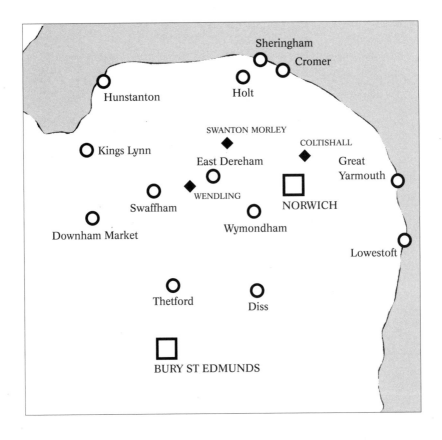

DEDICATION

I would like to dedicate this book to George Parnell, a true friend who gave much to his country in the Far East during WWII and who, I am sad to say, did not live to see this book.

Contents

1945

BETTY GRABLE A WARTIME FAVOURITE

Foreword

Some years ago I discovered, purely by chance, the diary of someone whom, I have since learned, was of remarkable character. With much persuasion, and only after agreeing to some very strict conditions, and a solemn pledge to be discreet regarding matters of identity, permission was given for me to publish edited extracts from what I shall henceforth refer to as 'Betty's diary'. The story of Betty is not unique; I have no doubt there were many such people, doing similar things in their own way throughout the Second World War on what is known as the 'Home Front'. People like Betty kept the spirit of a nation leavened with determination, a sense of what was right (something that was instinctive in Britain at the time) and a sense of humour that, while not making light of the appalling things that were happening in lands not.that far away – and at times looked as though they would be happening here (see the entries for May and June 1940 in particular) – managed to keep things in perspective. Although Betty settled well to her rural existence in Norfolk her years of travelling, and many years in London, were apparent in her 'we can take it' attitude – reminiscent of the 'London can take it' slogan during the very worst of the Blitz. London was a symbol of defiance to the world. One specific example of just how influential on events such a spirit was can be judged by the effect it had on one man: Ed Murrow, the American journalist who was in London during the worst of the bombing of 1940. Ed was often to be found on a roof somewhere giving a running commentary as the bombs fell about him. Such an effective broadcaster mobilised the spirit of a civilian population and sent it to war. Betty, and people like her, mobilised the spirit of the people they knew and were the personification of what it was that made the fight worthwhile. It would be a brave, foolish or ignorant individual who would deny that.

THE AMERICAN JOURNALIST
ED MURROW WITH
BROADCASTING HOUSE IN
THE BACKGROUND

THE FRIENDLY INVASION

Following the Japanese attack on Pearl Harbor, on December 7th 1942, it was inevitable that America would enter the war. Few could have predicted just how significant the American presence would be in East Anglia. The number of personnel was staggering, as was the might of the war machines they brought with them. That is too big a subject for me to go into here, however it is important not to let the sheer numbers get in the way of the sacrifice at a personal level. I am grateful to the family of Clyde Whitt for permitting me to quote here some records relating to his loss. It makes for grim reading but says a great deal about what the sacrifice of so many young men meant and how many lives were touched by the loss of a single plane.

USAAF MISSING AIRCREW REPORT #06523

Aircraft: #42-50287 (NO NICKNAME) 'V-Plus' 17th Mission
Aircrew: Larsen/Squadron: 577th

CREW POSITIONS AND STATUS

Pilot	I/Lt	Larsen, Niel R.	KIA
Co-pilot	2/Lt	Stratton, Charles R. Jr.	KIA
Navigator	2/Lt	O'Neill, Thomas J.	POW
Bombardier	2/Lt	Hiller, Thomas B.	POW
Nose gunner	PVT	Davis, Edward T.	POW
Radio operator	T/Sgt	Fox, Henry H.	POW
Engineer	T/Sgt	Robinson, William F.	KIA
Waist gunner	S/Sgt	Whitt, Clyde G.	KIA
Waist gunner	S/Sgt	Cristofaro, Gus J.	KIA
Tail gunner	S/Sgt	Prazak, Stanley J.	KIA

NEXT OF KIN DATA IN WWII:

Larsen	Wife, Arlene I., 3145, Forth Worth, Texas
Stratton	Wife, Virginia I., 816 North 24th St St. Joseph, Missouri
O'Neill	Father, Walter L., 4119 A Shaw Blvd, St. Louis, Missouri
Hiller	Mother, Margaret V., 6727 Toresdale Avenue, Philadelphia
Davis	Father, Gilbert W., Route #1, McMinnville, Tennessee
Fox	Wife, Frances K., 3115 Lincoln St, Columbia, South Carolina
Robinson	Mother, Emmie V., Eatonon, Georgia
Whitt	Mother, Mary Lee, Route #3, Roxboro, North Carolina
Cristofaro	Father, Joseph, 38 Oxford, Fernwood, Pennsylvania
Prazak	Mother, Antoinette C. 163 West Allen, Winsocki, Vermont

A **B-17 BOMBER** CREW

A LESSON FOR THE POLITICIANS

I am indebted to Betty for her care in preserving some newspapers and magazines from the war years. Each one seems to have been selected with care and to have a story that Betty found worth preserving.

In an issue of Picture Post, August 9th 1941, there is an article by J. B. Priestly which is, arguably, one of the finest pieces of writing produced for home consumption during the war. It is a classic example of a language being sent into battle, and was rightly described at the time as 'a valuable part of the record of Britain at War'. It was written after he had travelled 'thousands of miles up and down this island' and spent weeks talking with miners, dockers, soldiers, munitions workers etc. During that time it was inevitable that Priestly, being the man he was, would develop an insight into the state of the people of which it was worth taking note. All of what he says has the ring of truth; some is as relevant today as it was in 1941.

In the article – which was commissioned by Brendan Bracken – Priestly brings up a somewhat delicate question: 'What is it we are fighting for?' The question, in the context of the time, was not a stupid one. Priestly points out in his article that "it is not much use going into districts where there is only a tradition of frequent unemployment, bad housing, sadly restricted opportunity, and talking about 'our glorious heritage' and 'fighting to preserve our way of life'. Round there, they may not think much of our heritage and way of life. True, they could – and *would* – be much worse off under the Nazis, but many of these people can hardly be blamed for not understanding this. Meanwhile, we should stop trying to sell them heritages". Later in the same article Priestly makes the point that the government, with a total war on its hands was taking from the people various things such as taxes, leisure etc., and nobody minds; in fact the people have always been willing to make really gigantic sacrifices; but the government was making the mistake of taking without giving, having established a one-way track between itself and the people and becoming rapidly totalitarian in its demands; never having thought of trying to put back some of the colour it had taken out of life – being good at closing resorts, hotels, theatres, but no good at all at opening them. It never tried to make a fuss of the people, to give them some pleasant as well as unpleasant surprises. Priestly in no uncertain terms accused the government of suffering from a "shocking lack of imagination". I suppose in recent years this is not dissimilar to the financial hardships inflicted on the people of this country in times of recession; the 'medicine is foul but necessary' principle; all stick and not a nibble at a carrot. In my humble opinion any politician of modern times who did not take the trouble to ponder Priestly's views would be foolish in the extreme.

In a lighter vein – though not by much – Priestly comments on the orations at the time by various admirals and colonels pointing out "that there's a war on". Priestly makes it clear that "The ordinary folk of this country know very well that there is a war on. Some of them – the dockers, for example – have seen quite a lot of it already; wives who have to give their husbands a couple of slices of bread and margarine to take with them for a day's heavy work, *they* know there's a war on. Families that have been split up by enlistment and evacuation, *they know* there's a war on".

IMAGES OF WAR

I have tried to give a flavour of life in the six years of war by including some of the enduring images that would have been seen in magazines, newspapers and as posters. I wish I could have also included some of the evocative sounds of the time: that of a sky filled with Allied bombers: the Lancasters of the Royal Air Force, each with their four mighty Rolls Royce Merlin engines; the B17s and B24s of the USAAF 'Mighty Eighth' Bomber Group; the familiar voices of the announcers and newsreaders of the BBC such as John Snagge, Alvar Lidell, Wynford Vaughan Thomas, Richard Dimbleby, Wilfred Pickles and Jack Priestly to name just a few. Then there were the entertainers: Tommy Handley, Elsie and Doris Waters, Jack 'mind my bike' Warner, Arthur Askey, Stinker Murdoch – no stranger to Norfolk –and Tommy Trinder. Talking of the BBC: as far as morale was concerned its contribution was without measure or equal. Indeed, the BBC at war is worth a book all of its own. Broadcasting House, that most formidable of British 'battleships', in the harbour that is Langham Place. If Vietnam was the first 'television' war, then certainly WWII can accurately be called the 'radio war'.

A SNAPSHOT OF HISTORY

I have spoken to many who had relations in East Anglia during the period covered by Betty's diary. There is an enduring curiosity about life in those strange and dangerous times. That is why there are so many visitors every year to the region, many from the USA and other countries who were our allies. I hope, through this book, to give to the curious, and those who had family serving here, an idea of their lives then, and the people they met. I have found the whole project fascinating and can recommend to everyone the idea of researching further. Who knows, there may be other diaries and journals lying in attics all over the country, if not the world, deserving to be read and preserved.

Nicholas Webley

Introduction

This is Betty's story

At various times Betty lived in Coventry, London and many other places when she toured with various theatre and music hall companies. She had been a cook and back-room girl and seamstress at a number of theatres (the Holborn and Shepherd's Bush Empires and The Aldwych to name but three). In the early part of the century working the halls was a way of life to the likes of Betty, and it was clearly a world she sometimes missed.

When war broke out Betty was a widow. Her husband, Alfred, had died in the early nineteen-thirties; she was fifty-eight and had no children. From what I have been able to gather she resembled the actress Peggy Mount in physical appearance and manner. During this time Betty kept her journal, of sorts; in reality it is a large number of scraps of paper, backs of envelopes etc. (Regrettably the raw material of the diary had been stored in a shed since the war, and this has led to damage from damp, and the attention of rats and mice – I leave to your imagination the state in which I found it. Also with necessary handling, and because of the media used – i.e., pencil on low quality paper to hand at the time – most of the journal disintegrated, as I transcribed Betty's words, or was too unhygienic to keep or save.

With America's entry into the war Betty tried to make the American personnel feel at home; even going so far as trying her hand at cooking – although not often – with some of the exotic ingredients with which they supplied her.

The progress of the war was mentioned and how it was affecting her way of life and out-look. All this interspersed with personal notes – some of which are included but not all; some I have omitted because it was asked that I did not include them. Similarly, some of the names have been changed, but not all.

Since I began the task of assembling and annotating the journal I have often been asked who Betty really was and exactly where she lived. I will admit that I have been tempted to 'tell all' in moments of weakness. However, as I have got to know Betty, and the people she knew, through her sketchy and disintegrating notes and my own research, I have come to the conclusion that Betty was not just Betty: she spoke for a generation of people just like her. I have been told of others, from all over the country, who were similarly stalwart, inspirational and brave in the darkest of times. For this reason I have decided to leave Betty with a touch of mystery. Those who knew her knew her; that is all that matters. Anyway, curiosity killed the cat and Betty liked cats, and life can be enhanced by a little mystery.

APT WORDS FROM
WINSTON CHURCHILL

TIME FOR REFLECTION
BIG BEN LONDON

Timeline 1939-1945

1939

Sept 3   Britain, France, Australia and New Zealand declare war on Germany.

Sept 4   British Royal Air Force attacks the German Navy.

Sept 29   Germans and Soviets divide up Poland.

Nov 8   Assassination attempt on Hitler fails.

1940

Jan 8   Rationing begins in Britain.

March 16   Germans bomb Scapa Flow naval base near Scotland.

April 9   Germans invade Denmark and Norway.

May 10   Germans invade France, Belgium, Luxembourg and the Netherlands; Winston Churchill becomes British Prime Minister.

May 14   Local Defence Volunteers formed (later known as the Home Guard) 250,000 sign up within the first 24 hours.

May 15   Holland surrenders to the Germans.

May 26   Evacuation of Allied troops from Dunkirk begins.

May 28   Belgium surrenders to the Germans.

June 3   Germans bomb Paris; Dunkirk evacuation ends.

June 10   Norway surrenders to the Germans; Italy declares war on Britain and France.

June 14	Germans enter Paris
June 16	Marshal Pétain becomes French Prime Minister.
June 22	France signs an armistice with the Germans, dividing France in two: half occupied, half not, the latter being known as Vichy France.
July 10	Battle of Britain begins.
July 23	Soviets take Lithuania, Latvia and Estonia.
Aug 3-19	Italians occupy British Somaliland in East Africa.
Aug 13	German bombing offensive against airfields and factories in England.
Aug 15	Air battles and daylight raids over Britain.
Aug 17	Hitler declares a blockade of the British Isles.
Aug 23/24	First German air raids on Central London.
Aug 25/26	First British air raid on Berlin.
Sept 3	Hitler plans Operation Sealion (the invasion of Britain).
Sept 7	German Blitz against England begins.
Sept 11	Buckingham Palace hit – no casualties.
Sept 15	Massive German air raids on London, Southampton, Bristol, Cardiff, Liverpool and Manchester.
Sept 16	United States military conscription bill passed.
Sept 27	Tripartite (Axis) Pact signed by Germany, Italy and Japan.
Oct 7	German troops enter Romania.
Oct 12	Germans postpone Operation Sealion until Spring of 1941.
Oct 28	Italy invades Greece.
Nov	Germans bomb Coventry, Operation Moonlight Sonata.
Nov 20	Hungary joins the Axis Powers.
Nov 23	Romania joins the Axis Powers.

Dec 9/10	British begin a western desert offensive in North Africa against the Italians.
Dec 29/30	Massive German air raid on London resulting in what was known as the 'second great fire of London'.

1941

Jan 22	Tobruk in North Africa falls to the British and Australians.
Feb 11	British forces advance into Italian Somaliland in East Africa.
March 11	President Roosevelt signs the Lend-Lease Act.
April 6	Germans invade Greece and Yugoslavia.
April 14	Rommel attacks Tobruk.
April 17	Yugoslavia surrenders to the Germans.
April 27	Greece surrenders to the Germans.
May 10	Deputy Führer Rudolph Hess flies to Scotland.
May 10/11	Heavy German bombing of London; British bomb Hamburg.
May 24	HMS Hood sunk by the Bismarck.
May 27	Sinking of the Bismarck by the British Navy.
June 22	Germany attacks Russia.
June 28	Germans capture Minsk.
July 12	Mutual Assistance agreement between British and Soviets.
July 14	British occupy Syria.
Aug 14	Roosevelt and Churchill announce the Atlantic Charter
Sept 3	First experimental use of gas chambers at Auschwitz.
Sept 19	Germans take Kiev.
Sept 29	Germans murder 33,771 Jews at Kiev.
Oct 2	Operation Typhoon begins (German advance on Moscow).

Oct 16	Germans take Odessa.
Oct 24	Germans take Kharkov.
Oct 30	Germans reach Sevastopol.
Nov 13	British aircraft carrier Ark Royal is sunk off Gibraltar by a U-boat.
Dec 5	German attack on Moscow is abandoned.
Dec 7	Japanese bomb Pearl Harbor.
Dec 8	Britain and United States declare war on Japan.
Dec 11	Germany declares war on United States
Dec 16	Rommel begins a retreat to El Agheila in North Africa.
Dec 19	Hitler takes complete command of the German Army.

1942

Jan 1	Declaration of the United Nations signed by 26 Allied nations.
Jan 13	Germans begin a U-boat offensive along east coast of USA.
Jan 21	Rommel's counter-offensive from El Agheila begins.
April 16	Malta awarded the George Cross.
April 23	German air raids begin against cathedral cities in Britain.
May 8	German summer offensive begins in the Crimea.
May 26	Rommel begins an offensive against the Gazala Line.
May 27	SS Leader Heydrich attacked in Prague.
May 30	First thousand bomber British air raid (against Cologne).
In June	Mass murder of Jews by gassing begins at Auschwitz.
June 21	Rommel captures Tobruk.
June 25	Eisenhower arrives in London.
July 1-30	First Battle of El Alamein.

July 5	Soviet resistance in the Crimea ends.
July 9	Germans begin a drive toward Stalingrad in the USSR.
July 22	First deportations from the Warsaw Ghetto to concentration camps; Treblinka extermination camp opened.
Aug 7	British General Bernard Montgomery takes command of Eighth Army in North Africa.
Aug 12	Stalin and Churchill meet in Moscow.
Aug 23	Massive German air raid on Stalingrad.
Sept 2	Rommel driven back by Montgomery in the Battle of Alam Halfa.
Sept 13	Battle of Stalingrad begins.
Oct 18	Hitler orders the execution of all captured British commandos.
Nov 8	Operation Torch begins (U.S. invasion of North Africa).
Nov 11	Germans and Italians invade unoccupied Vichy France.
Nov 13	Tobruk captured by the Eighth Army.
Nov 19	Soviet counter-offensive at Stalingrad begins.
Dec 13	Rommel withdraws from El Agheila.
Dec 31	Battle of the Barents Sea between German and British ships.

1943

Jan 10	Soviets begin an offensive against the Germans in Stalingrad.
Jan 14-24	Casablanca conference between Churchill and Roosevelt.
Jan 23	Montgomery's Eighth Army takes Tripoli.
Jan 27	First bombing raid by Americans on Germany (at Wilhelmshaven).
Jan 30	First daylight raids on Berlin by RAF.

Feb 2	Germans surrender at Stalingrad in the first big defeat of Hitler's armies.
March 2	Germans begin a withdrawal from Tunisia, Africa.
March 16	Dambuster raids on the great dams of the Ruhr by Guy Gibson and 617 Squadron.
March 20-28	Montgomery's Eighth Army breaks through the Mareth Line in Tunisia.
April 6/7	Axis forces in Tunisia begin a withdrawal toward Enfidaville as American and British forces link.
May 7	Allies take Tunisia.
May 13	German and Italian troops surrender in North Africa.
May 16/17	British air raid on the Ruhr.
July 9/10	Allies land in Sicily.
July 19	Allies bomb Rome.
July 24	British bombing raid on Hamburg.
July 25/26	Mussolini arrested and the Italian Fascist government falls; Marshal Pietro Badoglio takes over and negotiates with Allies.
July 27/28	Allied air raid causes a firestorm in Hamburg.
Sept 8	Italian surrender is announced.
Sept 9	Allied landings at Salerno and Taranto.
Sept 11	Germans occupy Rome.
Sept 12	Germans rescue Mussolini.
Sept 23	Mussolini re-establishes a Fascist government.
Oct 1	Allies enter Naples, Italy.
Oct 13	Italy declares war on Germany; Second American air raid on Schweinfurt.
Nov 6	Russians recapture Kiev in the Ukraine.

Nov 18	RAF air raid on Berlin.
Nov 28	Churchill, Roosevelt and Stalin meet at Teheran.
Dec 24-26	Soviets launch offensives on the Ukrainian front.
Dec 26	Scharnhorst sunk.

1944

Jan 6	Soviet troops advance into Poland.
Jan 15	Eisenhower made Commander in Chief of Expeditionary Force as Operation Overlord – the invasion of Hitler's 'Fortress Europe' – is planned.
Jan 17	First attack towards Cassino, Italy.
Jan 22	Allies land at Anzio.
Jan 27	Leningrad relieved after a 900-day siege.
Feb 15-18	Allies bomb the monastery at Monte Cassino.
March 4	First major daylight bombing raid on Berlin by the Allies.
March 15	Second Allied attempt to capture Monte Cassino begins.
March 18	British drop 3,000 tons of bombs during an air raid on Hamburg, Germany. Cassino taken.
April 8	Soviet troops begin an offensive to liberate Crimea.
May 11	Allies attack the Gustav Line south of Rome.
May 12	Germans surrender in the Crimea.
May 15	Germans withdraw to the Adolf Hitler Line.
May 25	Germans retreat from Anzio.
June 5	Allies enter Rome.
June 6	D-Day landings in Normandy.
June 12	Churchill visits Normandy beach head.
June 13	First German V1 rocket attack on Britain.
June 27	US troops liberate Cherbourg.

July 9	British and Canadian troops capture Caen.
July 20	German assassination attempt on Hitler fails.
Aug 7	Germans begin a major counter-attack toward Avranches.
Aug 15	Operation Dragoon begins (the Allied invasion of Southern France).
Aug 19	Resistance uprising in Paris.
Aug 20	Allied encircle Germans in the Falaise pocket
Aug 25	Liberation of Paris
Sept 1-4	Verdun, Dieppe, Artois, Rouen, Abbeville, Antwerp and Brussels liberated by the Allies.
Sept 4	Finland and the Soviet Union agree to a cease-fire.
Sept 17	Operation Market Garden: British First Airborne Division landed at Arnhem.
Oct 14	Allies liberate Athens; Rommel commits suicide.
Oct 21	Massive German surrender at Aachen.
Oct 30	Last use of gas chambers at Auschwitz.
Nov 24	French capture Strasbourg.
Dec 16-27	Battle of the Bulge in the Ardennes.

1945

Jan 1-17	Germans withdraw from the Ardennes.
Jan 26	Soviet troops liberate Auschwitz.
Feb 4-11	Churchill, Roosevelt and Stalin meet at Yalta.
March 7	Allies take Cologne.
March 14	First ten ton 'Grand Slam' bombs used by RAF on Bielfeld viaduct.
April 1	Allied offensive in north Italy.
April 12	President Roosevelt dies. Truman becomes President.

April 16	Soviet troops begin their final attack on Berlin; Americans enter Nuremberg.
April 18	German forces in the Ruhr surrender.
April 21	Soviets reach Berlin.
April 28	Mussolini is captured and hanged by Italian partisans; Allies take Venice.
April 30	Hitler commits suicide.
May 2	German troops in Italy surrender.
May 7	Unconditional surrender of all German forces to the Allies.
May 8	VE Day.
May 9	Hermann Göering is captured by members of the U.S. 7th Army.
May 23	SS Reichsführer Himmler commits suicide; German High Command and Provisional Government imprisoned.
June 5	Allies divide up Germany and Berlin and take over the government.
June 18	Demobilisation in UK begins.
June 26	United Nations Charter is signed.
July 1	U.S., British, and French troops move into Berlin.
July 26	Atlee succeeds Churchill as British Prime Minister.
Aug 6	First atomic bomb dropped, on Hiroshima, Japan.
Aug 9	Second atomic bomb dropped on Nagasaki
Aug 14	Japanese agree to unconditional surrender.
Sept 2	VJ Day

List of main characters

Albert

Betty's much loved and well fed cat, some would say overweight, but not, if they had any sense, to Betty's face. He liked to lie in the sun on his barrel in summer and on his chair by the range in winter. A tabby and according to legend one of the largest there was.

Alfred

Betty's late husband. Had a cheeky smile 'like Max Miller'.

Fred Barnard

Did odd jobs and was a good garden carpenter. He was slightly older than Betty and was often seen out with his gun after rabbits, pigeons and the like. He came over as a bit heartless where animals were concerned but he wasn't as bad as he sometimes appeared. He was said to be a poacher, a likely tale (sic) and a suspicion never proved in court.

Billy 'I'

A member of the Aircrew (impossible to be more precise). He had a mother at home in Durham and two brothers who were at school. His father was in the Royal Navy. He was posted to Kent. His girlfriend was an aircraft plotter.

Edgar Brooks

A self-employed handyman and smallholder, his wife, Ethel, ran off in 1935/6 with a farm labourer and wasn't heard of again.

Daniel

A pig of Betty's acquaintance and much attached to Jennifer Medwin. He was often seen going for sedate walks with her, and occasionally with Betty.

Doris

The owner of the local shop where Betty helped out from time to time. Betty supplemented her income by baking cakes, scones etc., for sale in the shop and also for the Tea Rooms in Thetford where Doris had contacts by, possibly, marriage.

Mavis Emery

Helped at the pub and with baking if necessary. She was in her thirties.

French George

A business acquaintance of Freddie Walton with French connections and salt water in his veins. The full story of what this pair got up to has not been told – yet.

George

The local publican. He was married to Beryl, with a brother, Fred, who lived away. He liked boxing and the 'wireless' and tuned in around the world.

Mr Head

A veteran of the Great War. He was wounded in action and not very mobile at times and prematurely aged. He has bad legs and a wheezy chest through a mild gas attack.

Gordon Housego

A member of the Home Guard. Betty once had to tear him off a strip for flashing a copy of Picture Post around which had an article about what to do if the Germans had invaded Britain.

Jack

A close friend of Betty who lived just a few doors away. He was about the same age and a keen gardener who liked to shoot. He was a good provider of game throughout the war. He had a van and did the odd local delivery, carpentry etc. He was a Jack-of-all-trades, literally.

Catherine Jones

Introduced to Betty by Mrs. Wentworth. She was an Army nurse in her late twenties who was training girls in first aid.

Glim Jones

A singer and dancer Betty knew in London and, according to Betty, very attractive with a good voice. She worked in department stores when between theatrical engagements. She appeared in a number of reviews in theatres up and down the country.

Edie Maywick

Kept a boarding house in East Dereham (sometimes referred to as Dereham).

Jock Naylor

The local fishmonger.

Jennifer Medwin

A Land Army girl from Manchester who, according to Betty, had a 'good pair of legs'. She had a good job, which she gave up to get involved in the war effort. Her father was a well-to-do businessman with a position in local government and her mother helped out in a small private hotel.

Patricia

A friend of Glim who works at the BBC.

Gilbert and Marjorie Savage

Were local farmers of a largish farm. They had a son, Jim, in the army. Gilbert was unfortunate enough to break his leg in late October 1940.

Stanley

Betty's half-brother who lived in Clapham. Two years older than Betty he was single and not short of a bob or two. He was ex-Royal Navy.

Ted Sturgess

The local dealer in small quantities of timber and the like.

Tyke

A puppy who was, by any measure, most fortunate.

Harry Wainwright

Lived just outside Ilminster, Somerset. He had one of the best dog acts in the business. He gave Monty and Ruby, two terrier puppies to Betty and Mr Head.

Freddie Walton

A local black marketer, twenty-ish. He was a helpful boy and an indispensable person to those he supplied. He was always cheerful, but often reckless and a true entrepreneur. He failed his Army medical due to the after effects of a childhood illness, which he did not make public.

Mr and Mrs Wentworth

Had contacts at Whitehall/War Office. They were the owners of a large property and were frequently visited by VIPs. Mrs. Wentworth leaned politically to the left – much to the displeasure of her family. Betty frequently helped Mrs. Wentworth and was well accepted as a close family friend and most trusted confidante of both the Wentworths.

Jimmy West

A friend of Betty who lived in a village some miles away. He was from a poor family, and a most thoughtful and selfless individual.

PART ONE

'We are warriors all'

September 3rd 1939 – Christmas 1940

September 1939

SUNDAY 3rd

We are now at war with Germany. Jack and I were at the pub to listen to Mr. Chamberlain today. Like George said it has come as no surprise to any of us but we all hoped that it would not happen. Everyone went very quiet as the day went on. I suppose we are all wondering where it will all end. The King said on the wireless that there will be dark days to come.

MONDAY 4th

All the papers are full of the news: Britain's first day of war and the King's speech. It is a very serious war and I do not think that it will be over as quick as some people are saying. Jack has been saying for years that Hitler has been getting away with murder the way he has been building up his army, navy and air force. I thought he was being a misery but it turns out he was right all along. Jack nearly burst his braces in the pub tonight when he read in the Daily Sketch that Hitler had said the Poles had attacked Germany, not the other way round and the war was our fault. I have not read all the papers yet as I found it all too upsetting. I will keep them for a little while and look at them later. I called in to see Mr. Head and he was sure that it wouldn't be as bad as the last one.

WEDNESDAY 6th

Coal and electricity is to be rationed by a quarter from the weekend. I only have the light and the wireless on the electric and Jack sees I have plenty of wood for the range so I should be alright. I've told Jack that it will be a good idea if he eats some of his big meals round here as it doesn't cost any more to light a fire for two than it does for me on my own. I told Mavis the same. I asked about candles but nothing has been said about them being rationed.

 # October 1939

SATURDAY 7th

I overheard Mrs. Wentworth in the butcher's saying that her sister and brother-in-law are staying at the Maids Head in Norwich. They are both in uniform and stationed at different ends of the country so they are having their leave halfway. They are paying 17/6 a day for their room. That's a lot more than Alfred and I paid the last time I stayed in a hotel in '31. Mr. Head asked me to check if his blackout was alright as he has heard that he could go to prison or be fined if he is showing a light. He only has oil lamps anyway and hardly shows a light with just his curtains. I put his mind at rest which was the main thing. I want to see if I can get him a wireless from somewhere seeing as how he spends so much time on his own what with his bad legs and chest. Perhaps young Freddie can help.

HOME GUARD RECRUITMENT POSTER

SUNDAY 15th

Popped in to see Mr. Head on the way to church with Mavis this morning. He was very miserable. Someone had been filling his head with silly ideas about Germans invading before Christmas, I can guess who that was. I had a word with young Freddie Walton about getting him a wireless and he said he would see what he could do. George was in a right old state this afternoon as he could not work out how to fix the lights on his van for the blackout. He tried some blue paper but according to the constable that won't do and he gave him a copy of the regulations. George says that if he does what they say he will be the only one who does, and reckons that the law applies differently to some than to others and if he blacks-out his lights as much as the book says he will not be able to see where he is going anyway.

MONDAY 16th

Mavis tells me she has had a man round asking who he could buy logs from as he wanted to buy all he could to fill his lorry. I told Jack and he said that he had sent him packing as he could see that his little game was to buy up all the wood cheap and sell it dear when the coal runs out.

WEDNESDAY 18th

George had a stand up row with one of his customers who said that he thought he must be getting more than his fair ration of petrol because of the amount of times he has seen him out with his van, and that he can't see that he is only using it for essential trips as he is supposed to. George said that the customer was quite happy to stand there with a pint of beer in his hand which he had had to go and fetch and his one and sixpence was as good as the next man's. That seemed to shut him up. Stanley has asked me in a letter to go and stay with him for a few days before things get any more difficult. He says that travelling about might not be very easy later on. I think I will go, probably before the end of the month. Emily says that she'll see to Albert, she will spoil him so he will be quite happy. I could go and see Cissie Webster while I was there. I have not seen her since she got married again eight years ago.

THURSDAY 19th

The rumours about having to have our cats and dogs destroyed were wrong. It said in the paper that there is enough food for animals. Albert only eats what we leave, fish heads and leftovers anyway, as do most pets people I know have got.

SATURDAY 21st

Spent the day tidying the garden and clearing away some of the weeds and rubbish before the weather turns. Cleaned out Albert's barrel, it was full of his bits and pieces he likes to play with. I don't expect he will spend much time in it until the spring now. No doubt he will take up his position in his chair by the range for the winter. He has put on some weight this year.

SUNDAY 22nd

The sermon was about the Royal Oak. The vicar talked about someone he knows who was one of those killed. I have been so busy I have hardly had any chance to think about it. I can remember how worried we used to be when Stanley was at sea and there wasn't even a war on. I did not get a paper today as it was full of stories about the Germans so I just had a look at Emily's when I went to lunch at hers. She roasted a chicken.

WEDNESDAY 25th

I've written to Stanley to tell him I will be coming next Monday assuming I can get a train. I will go and see Cissie when I'm there as well. I called in to see George about Saturday and to tell him that Mavis and Jack will be going. Mavis said she will bake a cake and Jack said to let him know if any more pigeons were needed. We have decided to make a really good night of it and decorate the pub and back room. We could all do with cheering up. Met Alfred Stringer and his wife when I was shopping, they have taken in two evacuees, two boys from London, both eight years old. Alfred tells me it is five years since they moved to Lowestoft. He is in a reserved job at the docks. Next week we have someone coming to give us a talk on air raid precautions. I can't think why any German would want to bomb us here. Although as Jack said they may hit us by mistake, and he can remember a Zeppelin raid on Dereham during the last war.

KOLYNOS DENTAL CREAM
THE SMALL PRINT ON THIS POSTER
ASKS USERS TO RETURN USED
METAL TOOTHPASTE TUBES IN
ORDER TO RECYCLE THEM FOR THE
WAR EFFORT

THURSDAY 26th

Freddie stopped me in the street this morning and asked me to stay up
late tonight as he might have a surprise for me. He came round at half-
past eleven with six chickens. He says that they are good layers. He would
not take any money for them but said that he would not mind the odd
egg or two. We put them in the old shed for the night and Freddie said
he would come round tomorrow to build them a run and somewhere
to sleep.

FRIDAY 27th

Freddie came round just after eleven this morning with the trailer on his bike loaded with wood and wire-netting. He has built a lovely hut and run for the chickens in the part of the garden that catches the sun and is out of the wind. He is very clever with his hands. Jack showed me a casualty list that was in the paper a few days ago. It made my blood run cold seeing all those names. I spent the evening plucking and dressing pigeons. Winnie says we should allow one and a half pigeons each. Jack brought me some vegetables for the pies and he took some round to the pub. Mavis managed to bake two fruitcakes, as she was given some dried fruit. I made a fruit pie from some of my bottled plums and raspberries.

SUNDAY 29th

I didn't get to bed until two o'clock this morning. Everyone who said they were coming did. Young Freddie brought some bottles of wine, which both Mavis and I liked. That left more beer for the men. There was hardly any food left over and Mr. Head said it was the best pigeon pie he had ever tasted. He had too much of the strong stout and had a doze by the fire for about an hour. George moved the wireless into the room after supper and we had some music to dance to. It made a nice change to see everyone having a good time and almost forgetting about the war. I popped in to see if Mr. Head was alright this afternoon. He was brighter than I have seen him for weeks. He asked me to help him find a photograph he says he's got of him and Lord Gort who is Commander in Chief of the field forces. He says it was taken in 1925.

MONDAY 30th

I worked in the shop this morning as Doris had to go into Norwich to see a friend. The shelves are getting a bit empty because people are buying more than they need. I didn't let anyone have more than a bag of sugar at a time, that way there was enough for everyone. I have made a list of things for Mavis to remember about feeding Albert and the chickens. I told her she could stay here for the odd night if she felt like it, as it would help keep the place warm. Jack is picking me up at eight o'clock.

November 1939

Clapham

WEDNESDAY 1st

I don't think I would like to live in London for very long. It seems a lot closer to the war than at home. Stanley has taken me out to see some of the sights and tonight we went to his local. There was a lot of talk about the budget and income tax. We met some sailors on leave who Stanley knows and they were talking about a ship that had been sunk by a submarine.

SUNDAY 4th

I had a busy day clearing up and packing. I expect we will be leaving either tomorrow or the day after. Having an early night. My goodness it is cold tonight. I have had two hot water bottles and a fair old nip of the hard stuff to drive out the damp.

Back in Norfolk

THURSDAY 9th

The news today is not good. It looks as if the Germans will be in Holland very soon. If they are then Belgium could fall soon after. George says that Hitler wants to be able to attack us from the Dutch and Belgian coasts. We could have done without that kind of news. I made light of it all when Mavis came round as she does worry so and, as she spends a lot of time on her own, it can get her down. Jack has gone into Dereham to see someone at the Standard. I think he said they are trying to organise a darts match for next week. I sent three eggs to Mr. Head with Freddie this morning when he called with some food for the chickens. I told him that they were turning out to be very good layers. He said they came from a good strain and were well-bred hens.

FRIDAY 10th

Freddie left a note through the door saying that he wanted to see me tonight and would be popping in at half-past ten. Jack and me went to the pub for a drink and George had pinned up yesterday's paper. It had a headline about Hitler saying that he was ready for the war to last five years and then a bomb went off because someone tried to blow him up. There was something else in the paper about what happened to the Royal Oak. Poor Bob Bottomley was lost on that, and he wasn't even at sea. Mavis saw his wife and little boy only last week. Freddie came round to tell me he had managed to get a wireless for Mr. Head and he would like to take it round tomorrow morning. He would not take anything for it as he said it was a spare one.

FRIDAY 17th

Gladys came round today and was upset about her boy being called up. He's twenty-one and says he would prefer the navy to anything else. Even after the news from Scapa Flow he still wants to join.

SATURDAY 18th

Freddie has brought some boxes round for me to store for him as someone tried to break-in to his shed last night. He caught them at it and chased them away. I told him I heard a lorry going fast past here during the night and he said that it was probably them. I told him to be careful what he was up to as I am quite sure there are a lot of people who would like to get their hands on his goods. He is having some better locks fitted tomorrow and is moving his stuff back in the afternoon. I have finished all the blackout curtains now, so I should be getting paid for them this week. When I do I shall go into Norwich and buy some winter boots as mine are getting past their best.

SUNDAY 19th

Jack brought me some beef and kidney early this morning so I made a steak and kidney pudding for our dinner, and asked Mavis round as well. There was more than enough to go around and Jack said it was just the job on a damp old day like today. Freddie didn't come for his stuff. Fred Barnard sold me some kindling, two good cart loads which should last beyond Christmas. I went for a walk with Emily this afternoon and the leaves were a lovely colour. I don't like this time of year but it was a picture, even though it was very cold. Emily was quite sad as she had a letter from her cousin yesterday who is appearing in a pantomime, Cinderella I think she said, in London for Christmas at the Coliseum. Emily told me that it reminded her of when she used to do pantomime every year. The last one at the Lyceum in '35. She doesn't think she will do one again. I wondered why anyone should bother this year as there will not be many children in London to see it.

MONDAY 20th

Mrs. Wentworth said at the meeting tonight that as the news has been so bad just lately, it might be a good idea if we had the occasional talk about what was going on, so that people don't get upset and worried for no good reason. She said that the more people were informed, the less upset they would be when silly stories and rumours got about and they would themselves be able to improve morale. That made good sense to me as there have been some very long faces this last week, and it is much better for us all to face up to the truth than to worry about what could be nonsense. Mrs. Wentworth said she would try to get someone to give us a talk next week about the situation in Holland and Belgium, and how we may be able to help the war effort in our daily lives. After the meeting Mrs. Wentworth confided in me that she knows someone who met Hitler in Berlin a few years ago and she thought he was a silly little man, and that the people who were kow-towing to him were even more ridiculous, and whenever she hears bad news from abroad she thinks about that and knows that he is not made of the kind of stuff that wins a war against the likes of us.

TUESDAY 21st

Jack came round early this morning and told me that Freddie has not been seen anywhere since I last saw him. I do hope he's alright. I haven't said anything to anyone about having his goods round here, or about the people who he caught.

WEDNESDAY 22nd

Freddie turned up this morning to pick his goods up. I told him we had been worried about him and he said that he had gone into Norwich to sort out the people who had tried to break in to his shed. It had been the same people who he had bought some of his goods from and the man he had paid had not passed the money on but had kept it for himself. Albert has been in the garden most of the day which is unusual for him at this time of year.

December 1939

THURSDAY 21st

Doris had a delivery of cod roes in tins today. Seven dozen tins. She said they will make a good and nourishing breakfast now that bacon is scarce. I thought that it must have been a mistake for her to have been able to get so many tins at once but she told me she had ordered them and was expecting the same again in a fortnight. I bought six tins to put in the store cupboard as we could have some bad weather soon and they will come in handy. Mavis had the same as she has a recipe that she has wanted to try out. Stanley wrote to say he will be coming tomorrow. His letter has been in the post for five days. He is bringing some things with him even though I told him there was no need.

FRIDAY 22nd

Stanley arrived just after 11o'clock this morning looking very well. He had a good old chinwag with Mr. Head tonight, telling him about what it's like in London in the blackout, and showed him his cuttings from the London papers about the Graf Spee, him being an old merchantman he takes an interest. Mr. Head told us that his father was a sailor, I didn't know that. The ship on his sideboard is a model of his father's ship and I had never realised. Stanley saw him home and we both had a drink and an early night. Stanley likes my roast pheasant so I will do him one after Christmas before New Year. The pheasants for the party will be nice and gamey by now and not the way he likes them.

SATURDAY 23rd

The turkey is one of the best I have seen and will be just right. It looks as though there will be at least twenty for Christmas dinner and more for tea. Jack, Mavis and Fred Barnard came round for supper tonight and we all had a good drink and a laugh. Fred told us about some of his nights out with his gun. He had had rather too much to drink by then and I told him he should be more careful about what he says. He says that he was taught all he knows about poaching by his dad and grandad and they did more good than harm as they help to look after the young birds for nothing. His grandad told him that the owner of the land where he used to walk would give him two new pound notes every Easter for services rendered and used to tell his keepers that he was to be left alone. Not like today, because Fred still has some shot in him that he caught when a keeper tried to give him a fright two or three years back. Mavis asked him if he would take her out with him on one of his walks. She had had a bit too much sherry by then I think. The sherry was a present from the vicar for helping him with the apples this year. I had wrapped the pheasants for Fred to deliver tomorrow in time for Christmas. He has also given me some pigeons for New Year pies. It was Christmas Eve when everyone left and Stanley and I drank a toast to a happy Christmas.

HAPPY CHRISTMAS 1939

CHRISTMAS EVE

Mavis and I packed some Christmas boxes for some friends. A cooked pheasant, a Christmas pudding, and some mince pies for Mr. Head because that is what he said he would like, and Freddie asked us to put in a bottle of Haig that he brought round. Most of the others got mince pies and small puddings. We tried to give a little more to those who are not coming to the party. Ted has taken a really nice tree to the pub and Emily and George's wife decorated it today. I gave them a hand when I popped in to sort some things out in the back room for tomorrow. Fred Barnard brought two loads of holly and ivy and gave some to me. Stanley has put it all round the room and in the hall, and decorated our tree. Mavis and I had a busy day delivering boxes and things and helping with the children's party at the Wentworths's. Peter Wentworth made a good Father Christmas. There were a few sad faces on the evacuees who I suppose were homesick. Most cheered up though and all in all it was a happy do. Mavis invited Stanley, Jack and me round for a drink. We got home at half past twelve. It is Christmas Day. The first, and I hope the last, of the war.

CHRISTMAS DAY

Meat was not a problem, Betty's friend Jack saw to the turkey, he had several he was fattening. There would be twelve people sitting around the dinner table at the pub that Christmas, so Fred Barnard set to with his gun to obtain some pheasants; just to make sure there would be enough to go around. George, the landlord of the pub, saved the odd barrel, crate of local stout and bottle of whisky for the planned festivities.

All twelve of us sat down for dinner at 2 o'clock. It was a lot of work but everyone mucked in and it was well worth it. Mr. Head really enjoyed himself talking over old times with Stanley and young Freddie. We did all we could to forget our troubles and didn't listen to the news all day which made a change. A Christmas to remember and I am ready for my bed.

January 1940

MONDAY 1st
NEW YEAR'S DAY

This is the first time I have had to myself since Christmas. I have spent the whole evening writing letters. I had a long letter from Glim (Glim Jones, a singer Betty knew in London), she told me she was in a show at the Coliseum last year and now that things are as they are she is looking around for something else. She says she's thinking of joining up. I can't see Glim in uniform though, not with her background. Doris is worried that she may have trouble with working out the ration. What will we do about jams and things? I get through quite a lot in the course of a week, Mavis and I worked it out. Doris is getting hold of some recipes this week to help us manage without so much butter.

THURSDAY 4th

I shall be glad when spring comes. These dark mornings make every thing seem worse than it is. Jack and I went to the pub last night and everyone seemed very gloomy. George said that everyone was feeling flat after Christmas and that it was the same every year only made worse this year by the war.

FRIDAY 5th

I went with Jack to Dereham Standard. He had to see someone about some work. I had a chat with Edie Maywick who runs the boarding house and she asked me if I was available for a cooking job in Norwich at the end of the month. A family she knows is having some important guests and Doris can't do it as she is alone at home now. I said that I would think about it and let her know.

MONDAY 8th

It is a very cold day and I have hardly ventured outside. Albert went outside for about half and hour and has spent the rest of the day by the range. Fred says that he thinks we are in for some bad weather in a couple of weeks and is stocking up just in case. I asked him to put a few birds away for me in return for some baking. Freddie came round and told me he had been to see Mr. Head with a few things and brought me some chicken food for which he wanted nothing but I gave him some eggs.

TUESDAY 9th

The people who Edie Maywick told me about left a message for me at the pub to ring them. They asked me if I would be able to cook for them on Saturday February 3rd. It will mean staying the Friday night to help get everything ready. They are paying me two pounds ten shillings. I could not say no. They are sending me a menu. They will provide everything I need. I asked Mavis to give me a hand for half the money and she said she would. She has been working very hard arranging parcels of woollens for the Navy.

THURSDAY 11th

Poor old Jack. His van broke down in Watton today and he has spent the whole day trying to get it mended. He telephoned a chap he knows at Chapman's in Norwich and he took him a spare part and fitted it for him on the side of the road. It was gone seven o'clock before he got home and he was frozen. I had stew and onion soup on the range and I put in some dumplings. He soon recovered. We are going to Dereham market tomorrow as Jack is after some chickens but does not hold out much hope as he is sure they will be too dear.

FRIDAY 12th

Well, we went to Dereham but did not spend much time at the market. Jack saw someone he knows from Kirby Bedon who works for a poultry breeder. He asked us to meet him round the back of the Kings Arms with the van. He put four baskets in the back and we came home. They are lovely looking birds especially the cockerel. As Jack said he could never have afforded to buy them normally.

SATURDAY 13th

I went to the Collins's (owners of the 'big house') tonight. Their maid came round with a note this afternoon. Their cook had a fall and couldn't cook for a party of people they have staying for the weekend. It was only a simple meal for eight. Roast chicken and vegetables with cheese and biscuits. They were a very serious lot of guests. Service people from what I heard and what the staff told me. One of them was a Navy man and he was getting very angry at one stage about what happened to the Exmouth last month and the Royal Oak. He had been there (Scapa Flow) just before and knew many of those lost. Richard Collins (son of the Collins's) was back from wherever it is he goes. I often hear questions about why he isn't in uniform but he talks as if he is and I think he is involved in war work of some kind. He has always been very clever. When I left after clearing away at gone midnight Richard and one of the guests were playing chess in the big drawing room. Mrs. Collins gave me a lift home. This has been a good week for money one way and another. Jack has put one of his new chickens in with mine as the others keep pecking her.

POSTERS DEMONSTRATING THE CONSEQUENCE OF CARELESS TALK

February 1940

FRIDAY 2nd

Freddie is giving me and Mavis a lift into Norwich, I am just taking my knives and apron as everything else is provided. I am to cook a baron of beef with all the trimmings followed by pears poached in brandy.

SUNDAY 4th

I didn't get back until gone eleven o'clock this morning with Jack. The dinner went very well and Mrs. Sheridan paid me handsomely and was very pleased. Her guests included some directors of Mr. Sheridan's bank in London, her parents, Mr. Dunbar from Pickwilliam's Stores in Newmarket and his wife. I was invited to have coffee after the guests had left and Mr. Sheridan let me see a book he is writing about Sir Astley-Cooper, the famous surgeon who was born in Norfolk. The book is actually about the Paston family who everyone has heard of. There are some very old engravings of Sir Astley-Cooper that must be very old. Mavis did more than her share and was a great help.

THURSDAY 8th

I got up early to sort out the long pod and broad bean seeds. I have been meaning to do it for ages. I expect to have to sow late and I don't want to waste any time getting things in. I want to grow more turnips this year as they are good to store. I will put them near the artichokes. Fred always says that turnips, carrots and spinach grow best in ground where artichokes do well.

DIG FOR VICTORY POSTER TO ENCOURAGE
SELF SUFFICIENCY

March 1940

TUESDAY 5th

Mavis came round and we spent the best part of the day sowing vegetables. We managed to get in summer cabbage, some of Fred's carrots that he swears by, cauliflowers and six good rows of parsley right across the bottom of the garden. The sun was quite warm at times and rather cheering. Fred came and watched us while he leant on his stick and imparted some of his wisdom. There is not much he doesn't know about gardening. He never wastes an inch of his garden and if I can do half as well as he does I will be well pleased. He said he will sow some leeks, radishes and broad beans for me later in the month. His back was playing him up today as he said with a wink that he had been out all night. I found six pigeons hanging in the outhouse after he had gone.

SUNDAY 10th

I'm putting Fred's pigeons to good use by making pigeon pies for dinner today. Mavis has plucked them and cut them up. They are nice birds. There is enough for Mavis, Jack, Fred and me, and more than enough to make a good size pie for Mr. Head. He could not come himself today as he was at Stanley's (Prescott, an old friend of Mr. Head) for the day. I can make some tasty soup with the pigeon carcasses. It would have been nice for the boys next weekend but it won't keep. Jack fixed the netting on the chicken house this afternoon. He said it looks as though a fox has been trying to get in. It's a good thing that Freddie put a wire netting floor over the bottom otherwise I would have lost the lot.

TUESDAY 12th

I have spent the afternoon at the pub. George was moving some barrels in the pub cellar and one of them rolled on to his foot, and then he strained his back trying to roll it off to quickly. Mrs. Wentworth had a look at his foot and said that there were no bones broken as far as she could tell and strapped it up for him. I have told Beryl that I would be happy to help out until he is up and about again. Poor old George. It's what comes of being in too much of a hurry. I had a letter from Cissie. Both her lads have been sent overseas and her youngest brother has just been home on embarkation leave so it looks as if he'll be off as well soon.

WEDNESDAY 13th

I had a couple of hours in the garden this morning as it was quite sunny. Albert slept all day on his barrel so it must mean spring is here. I sowed all the onion seed Fred gave me so I should have about four times as many as last year. Fred has started making dog kennels. I gave him a picture of one I cut out of a magazine and he said he could make one just as good. He showed it to me today when I took him a cake. He has made a really good job of it. It is for a dog about the size of a Labrador with a porch at the front for the dog to lie down on, overlapping strips of wood on the roof to keep out the rain and cork in all the joints to keep out the draught. He also painted it to make it waterproof. He has orders for two more from a man he knows on Norwich market.

SATURDAY 16th

I delivered the cakes to the shop before seven this morning and then helped Mavis with her garden. She has dug all her flower beds up except for the bulbs and a bit of her lawn where it catches the sun best. We sowed spinach across the bottom of her garden right up to the ditch. I found no end of clay pipes. Fred says that part of Mavis's garden used to be part of a footpath that ran from where the old brew house used to be and the men used to stop at the old stump for a smoke.

SUNDAY 17th

It is a great worry to hear that Scapa Flow has been attacked. As well as all the boys from around here, Stanley and I know many who are likely to be there at the moment. Stanley has always had a horror of drowning even though he spent so long at sea. As he said, when he went to sea jobs were few and far between and he had little choice. I listened to the Forces Service on the wireless tonight for any more news but as I had promised to see Mr. Head I missed it. I baked some pasties for Jack to take tomorrow, if he has a lot of hard work to do at Howard's he will need more than sandwiches and tea. I baked a few extra for the shop and the pub. Mabel Huckley was in church today and if looks could kill. I wonder what she thinks I've done? Funny woman.

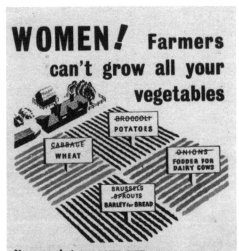

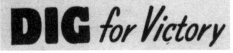

DIG FOR VICTORY POSTER
SHOWING THE IMPORTANCE OF
SELF SUFFICIENCY

MONDAY 18th

Although vegetables must come first this year I am determined to keep my flower beds in good order. The crocus bulbs I planted in the Autumn look lovely but the tulips are a real disappointment, I must ask Mrs. Wentworth what she thinks as hers are much better. I spent an hour or two digging out the daisies and weeds from the little lawn and raked the gravel path. Fred came and did some digging. We had toad in the hole for lunch with roast potatoes, carrots and tinned peas. I had a letter from Chummy Young. He's home on leave, well not at home exactly but in barracks. He says he's alright and that his sister has been sent to a factory in the midlands, she had volunteered for the Air Force and was very disappointed. Three cooking jobs this week, two of them at the Wentworth's and one for a friend of Mrs. Wentworth. Some of the family's shooting friends are staying for a few days. Heaven knows what they'd like to eat, they usually like game but this is not the time of year. I have an idea of my own.

TUESDAY 19th

An early start this morning. George had to go to Norwich and called round to see if I would like to go with him. As he was to be back by two o'clock I went as I had to be at the hall at three. We cleared out the stove and lit a roaring fire to make sure the chimney did not need sweeping. Jack said that he would stock up the wood shed in good time this year so that there won't be a rush as in most years. When I got home I found that young Freddie had left me some chicken feed and some tins of jam. Roly poly for Sunday I think.

WEDNESDAY 20th

Mrs. Wentworth came round just after nine to see about dinner tomorrow. I suggested cooking my steak and kidney pudding. I was surprised when she said it was a good idea. Apparently one of her guests – she called him the Major – always had steak and kidney pudding or pie at his London club. So that is what I will cook. She is getting the meat and suet so all I have to do is make it. Friday they are having trout.

THURSDAY 21st

Went to Wymondham today with Freddie in a van he had borrowed for a few days. As I walked through the market place I saw a man beating his dog with a stick. I took it off him and hit him with it and he ran off like a frightened rabbit, all six feet of him. I told him he was not fit to have a dog and brought it home. I recognised him. It was that Ted Tyler, a real bad lot. Jack had to square him up about how he was treating some chickens last year. It is a lovely dog. Jack thinks he is a Labrador cross. He is very mild tempered and doesn't frighten Albert one bit. They were eating out of the same bowl tonight. Jack says that he will ask the Howard's if they would like him. He deserves a good home like that. He answers to Bob, so it seems it must be his name or something similar. He is asleep by the fire as I write this.

FRIDAY 22nd

A happy ending. Jack took Bob to the Howard's and they said they would be glad to give him a home. They have two Labradors already and Jack said they got along really well together. Only Jack and I know where he is and where he came from so he should be alright from now on. I did tell young Freddie about Tyler beating his dog and he said he had no time for any of that family as they were always ready to do anyone down, and Ted was the worst of the lot.

SATURDAY 23rd

Billy 'I' came to see me this morning. His girlfriend, Sarah, is coming over this afternoon and staying with Mavis for the weekend. He's told us all so much about her it will be nice to see what she is like. Had some extra baking for the shop. Helped out at the pub. Quite a few of the boys in tonight from 'C'. Jack was quite pleased as he had a good night with the darts and hardly paid for a drink all night.

SUNDAY 24th

Billy and Sarah came for lunch and as it was a special occasion I cooked roast beef and Yorkshires. It may be some time before I see Billy again as he has been posted.

April 1940

As Norway is Great Britain's neighbour a shiver went down the spine of everyone as the news from there worsened...

WEDNESDAY 10th

A bright spring day to help lift some of the gloom caused by the news from Norway. Fred came round and planted the potatoes he promised. I must remember to keep them earthed up. I could not help him in the afternoon as I had a couple of hours giving Beryl a hand clearing out the two upstairs back-rooms at the pub as she wants to start letting them. She has been asked quite a few times in the last couple of months by people who are staying in the district for a day or two and who would prefer a pub to a hotel. Beryl asked if I would be prepared to help with the cooking and extra cleaning for the guests when they are busy and said that I could have a firm arrangement if I would like one and take a share of the letting income. I said "yes" like a shot. I stayed very late at the pub last night as the news came in from Norway. Will this bad news never end? There does not seem to be anything we can do to stop the Germans doing what they want and going where they feel inclined. And when the Navy do their best by mining the sea to keep them out people talk about mining territorial waters. Someone had better start doing something about all this or we will be next. According to Mrs. Wentworth's paper the Germans have been planning this (the invasion of Norway) for months and they have been helped by Nazi agents who were already in Norway. That sent a shiver down my back, it really did, especially what it said how the towns that resisted the Germans were bombed. What kind of people are they, bombing innocent civilians like that. Would this country surrender if our cities were to be bombed like that? I would rather not think about that.

THURSDAY 11th

Finished off clearing the rooms at the pub. I had not realised what a nice view they have across the fields from the windows. They are quite good-sized rooms and the next job will be to get them fitted out and comfortable. There were two bedsteads in the old washhouse that will look good with a bit of elbow grease on the brass and I have a wardrobe that I never use which Jack is taking for me tomorrow. If we stick at it we should have both rooms ready by next Monday.

FRIDAY 12th

The rooms are finished. Mavis was a great help and put up the curtains and by the time we came away tonight both rooms looked a picture. We managed to end up with two double rooms and a small single. I told Beryl that those two rooms would be a great asset to the pub.

SATURDAY 13th

Well that didn't take long. We have let one of the rooms for next week to one of Alec Mills' daughters who is spending some leave here, good old Doris. Freddie dropped off some bent tins that came his way and said that if I insisted he would be happy to accept half a dozen eggs as payment. There was a rare old mixture: baked beans, corned beef, peas, peaches, a dozen tins of tomatoes, eight huge tins of foreign jam, pears cherries, apples, raspberries and pineapple. And none of the tins are that badly dented. I must make sure I put such bounty to good use.

KITCHEN WASTE
EVERYTHING HAS VALUE

SUNDAY 14th

I went to church this morning much cheered by the news about the Navy's victory off the coast of Norway. They certainly gave the Jerries a bloody nose that will make them think. I bet Stanley is pleased. Mrs. Wentworth said that she thought this was a turning point of a kind. I had to stop to help Mr. Head home so I didn't have as long to talk with her as I would have liked. Jack and Fred came for lunch. I cooked a chicken Jack bought at the Market yesterday. Albert had a bad cough so I have kept him in the warm and tonight he seemed much better. I am helping out at the pub tomorrow as Evelyn Mills is arriving and we want to make sure everything is ship shape for our first guest. I had a letter from Maurice Isaacs saying he's putting on a show in the West End in the summer all being well. He just wrote to ask how I was and to send me an autographed photograph of Tom Walls. He is staying in the same digs as I did when I was at the Empire. He said he had been in Birmingham for nine months and it had been a dead loss as far as work was concerned. Since he's been back in London he's been at it all the time.

MONDAY 15th

The news from Norway is not good, and doesn't bear thinking about. What we need to hear is some good news to raise our spirits. At the meeting tonight we had a talk by Mrs. Freeman about reducing waste in the home, kitchen and garden and we were all asked to come up with ideas. Mine was to not throw away the outside leaves of cabbages. If you just boil them for a few minutes you can make parcels of meat and vegetables and cook them in stock in the oven and make a very nourishing meal. My mother said that during the potato famine in Ireland nothing was thrown away and this was one of her mother's ideas. Jack heard in the pub tonight that the police have arrested Ted Tyler after finding some stolen tyres in his shed. Apparently he said someone put them there to get him into trouble. A likely story. Serves him right for what he did to poor Bob. I must remember to ask young Freddie for some more chicken feed.

WEDNESDAY 17th

We are off on one of our long walks this Saturday. Mavis says that it is over a year since our last one. Emily and Arthur are coming along with Freddie and Edgar. We will walk the six miles by the meadow, along the river, over the bridge to the beekeeper's wood and straight down the hill to Fiddler's Pond where we will stop to eat. We'll walk home around the old keeper's cottage past the old railway carriage, down through Lallycote Lane along the big ditch and home. That's the long walk we had the year before last.

THURSDAY 18th

Had a morning at Mrs. Wentworth's making up the beds in four of the bedrooms. She has guests coming tomorrow for the weekend. She was not her usual self and seemed worried about something. She said to me in confidence that she had heard, from a friend of her husband's in London, that things were not looking very good in the Netherlands. She said the government are worried that what will happen in the next few weeks will be very bad for morale, and morale was what can make the difference between victory and defeat. I helped Doris in the shop this afternoon and had an enquiry about a room at the pub. This evening I caught up on some sewing, my People's Friend and listening to the Forces network.

MAKE-DO AND MEND
A STITCH IN TIME SAVES 9d

FRIDAY 19th

I have made up a picnic for Mavis, Freddie and me. I am quite looking forward to it, although I don't know about the weather. I called in on Mr. Head to see if there was anything he wanted doing, and would you believe he was digging his garden like a boy of eighteen. He said that he hasn't felt so fit for ages and that his cold seems to have done him some good. I made him a meat and potato pie, a jam tart and put it in his oven. Jennifer Medwin has some time off and is coming along on the walk as well.

SATURDAY 20th

The long walk

We started at about half past ten. Jennifer, Mavis and I picked up the others and off we went. It was just the right weather for it too. Fred, although he does not look as though he can, can out walk all of us. Young Freddie told me that he bets he walks more than five miles most nights that he's out with his gun, and practise makes perfect. Jennifer looked very pretty and it seemed funny for her not to be in her uniform. She certainly is a head-turner. I told her she would make a good principal boy in panto with those legs of hers. We stopped for our picnic at about two o'clock and took our time walking home. We stopped at the pub and stayed until about ten. We had a really nice day and we've got two more bookings for next week, one for two days and one for three. What with one thing and another it looks as though I will have a busy time.

EVACUATE! A BRITISH CIVIL DEFENCE POSTER

May 1940

**A long, harrowing, month. The Germans took more of our neighbours':
Holland, Belgium and Luxembourg. Conscription age went up to 36.
A quarter of a million enrolled in the Local Defence Volunteers – in
one day. On Sunday May 26th what came to be known as the 'miracle'
of Dunkirk got under way – a display of courageous collective action
by ordinary people unsurpassed in history.**

THURSDAY 9th

Jack asked me if I would like to go to the pub tomorrow night as George
is sure he can get a boxing match on his wireless. Lou Ambers is fighting
a man called Jenkins in America. I know that because Jack has always
been interested in boxing and used to be quite good at it when he was
in the army. No letter from Stanley, a week late.

FRIDAY 10th

Mrs. Wentworth came very early this morning before most people had
heard any news. She told me that she had had a telephone call from a
friend at the War Office and that he had told her the Germans had invaded
Holland and Belgium. She said that she wanted to stop people from
being frightened as much as possible. As she had said at meetings many
times, invading countries across the channel is a lot different than trying
to invade us this side of it. She asked me to try to calm down anyone
who may be very upset by the news when they hear it. In confidence
she told me that it was expected that there would be some very good
news by the end of the day but she could not say exactly what. Everyone

has been listening to the wireless and this evening we heard that Chamberlain had gone and Winston Churchill is the new Prime Minister. This was the good news that Mrs. Wentworth was no doubt talking about. She has never liked the way Chamberlain has handled things. She has always said that the way to deal with a bully is not to give them what they want but what they need, a damn good hiding. I had a word with Mavis and told her to try to keep her spirits up.

THE CHANNEL A BOUNDARY REQUIRING CONSIDERATION

SATURDAY 11th

Just got back from the pub. I didn't stay for the fight. All I could hear on the wireless was a lot of whistling and scratching. George said he was sure his aerial was long enough but as the fight didn't start until late I came home. Edgar Brooks had too much to drink and started creating about the Whitsun bank holiday being cancelled. Jack said he was daft as he worked for himself and could take it off anyway if he wanted to and no one would be any the wiser. Poor old Edgar stood there with his mouth open and didn't know what to say. We worked out that it must be nigh on five years since his Ethel ran off with that farm labourer. I wonder where she is now. She never wrote. I'm having six for lunch tomorrow.

CHURCHILL
GALVANISING THE NATION

SUNDAY 12th

Three boys from 'C' today. Mr. Head came too and was in his element. As Johnny 'H' said this has been quite a week one way and another, what with the invasion of Holland, Luxembourg and Belgium, and Churchill taking over. The talk at 'C' is that he is more of a war leader than Chamberlain. Mr. Head said that he has made a good start by having a government with all the best brains from all the parties.

UNDATED

Mr. Churchill's speech made my blood run cold. It made me realise just how much trouble we could be in for. I suppose the only thing to do is to look after our own and do our bit as much as we can. What else can we do here? If we can grow what we can and try not to use up our stocks of things that come from abroad or, like coal and the like, things that are needed for the war effort we will be doing all that we can. Emily came round for some of my cough mixture as her Arthur is full of the cold again. He seems to pick up anything that's going, poor chap.

THURSDAY 16th

Jack has been saying for ages how he wished he could do a bit more and today he is full of the news about the Local Defence Volunteers. He is going to sign up as soon as he can. So is Fred, young Alfie Morris, George and a few others I should not wonder. I have said that I will help out if I can and Mrs. Wentworth has offered them the use of her barn if they need it.

UNDATED

These are the darkest days so far. It is very hard to keep your chin up when the news is so bad. I think it is a lot worse than we are being told. One of the boys was telling me this afternoon that from what he has heard the Germans will drive us out of France within days. Much the same as Mrs. Wentworth has said.

UNDATED

Mr. Head asked Jack to see if there was any way he could be in the LDV as he served from 1914 to 1918 and he's sure he could teach them a thing or two. It seems a shame that he can't join as he is so keen to help.

June 1940

The 'phony war' seemed an age ago, as the war proper got underway. The evacuation of Dunkirk had focussed the mind of the nation on the narrowness of the English Channel. The Battle of France commenced, and the Nazi stain spread – seemingly unstoppable. To confuse any uninvited visitors signposts were removed where it was thought strategically prudent. In Norfolk a survivor of the Dunkirk beaches arrived at Betty's door.

LATE MAY EARLY JUNE

It is very hard to know what to think. We hurry around doing the best we can with what we have and yet we don't seem to be getting anywhere. After the invasion of Holland and Belgium it looked as if we would be next. Mavis said that she was sitting near some soldiers in the cafe in Norwich the other days and they were saying how the b-Belgians had betrayed us. They surrendered without warning and left us open to attack on the other side. If our friends let us down who can we rely on? Now the BEF have had to be brought home in lots of little boats as the Navy could not cope on their own. It is obvious from what is on the news that things are not going our way. I hope Jack is right when he says that the reason we had to get out of Dunkirk quick was so that we can go back again and that it won't be long before we do. Mr. Wentworth said much the same thing, that to be able to organise something on that scale shows the rest of the world that we are far from finished. That is all very well but when we hear on the news and read in the papers that the Germans have sent us packing it makes everyone fearful of what might happen next. Jack says that the main job the LDVs have to do is look out for enemy parachutists. They have all been issued with armbands and later they should have full uniforms and equipment. Mavis and I are going to help sort things out at the hall for their meeting on Sunday and make the teas. Although as Mavis said, we have enough to do as it is without having to be LDVs as well.

A FAMILY EMERGING FROM THEIR 'ANDERSON SHELTER'
ALL ANDERSON SHELTERS HAD TO BE ERECTED BY JUNE 11 1940, OTHERWISE 'SUBSTANTIAL PENALTIES WOULD BE IMPOSED'.

WEDNESDAY 5th

It looks as though most of the BEF are back home now. It sounds as though they made a very sad sight. Two cooking jobs today as well as helping in the pub this evening. I am ready for my bed.

THURSDAY 6th

Had a letter from Mauri. He has sent me a long list of all the old crowd and where some of them are. He tells me he saw Glim in May at an audition for a singing job. His letter has brought back some memories: how the Simms twins got drunk and hung all their landlady's washing under the pier because she wouldn't give them a key to the front door, and the day Jimmy Nervo shared his umbrella with me on the way to a matinee. And poor old Dunsford Kelly, I wonder where he is now, Mauri says he hasn't seen him since '35 in Wrexham. I remember that one night after a show I was having a drink with Dunsford and he had had more than his fair share but that was Dunsford for you, and he said he would show me something that few other people had seen. He swore me to secrecy. He opened his case and under a false bottom he took out a thick cardboard folder and handed it to me. It was on old piece of paper with faded brown writing on it that I could not easily read. Dunsford said it was a complete page from Twelfth Night in Shakespeare's own hand. It was given to him by an old actor he met when he was a boy, and he had carried it with him ever since. He did a reading from it for me which was something like: 'I am not weary and it is long to night'. Dear old Dunsford, he was a real gentleman and always raised his homburg to a lady.

MONDAY 10th

Freddie came round this evening with a little dog, he has been away for a few days down south. He said that he got caught up with all the troops coming back. He seemed to be rather shocked by it all and he said that it was the first time he had seen so many people in uniform and that there was a lot of them wounded. One of them he had talked to who had just got off the boat had brought the little dog back with him. He had found him lying under a burnt out lorry and he wasn't very old, hardly ten weeks I would think. The soldier asked Freddie to take it with him as any dogs or cats brought back had to be destroyed and did not want to see that happen to little Tyke, as he called him, as they had both got back after Hitler had had a good old go at stopping them. Freddie said that he had a good home lined up for him in Attleborough and he asked me to give the little chap some food. I minced him some beef with bread and gave him a big bowl of milk. After he had fallen asleep Freddie popped him back in his basket and left. He is taking him to Attleborough early in the morning. I told him his secret was safe with me.

TUESDAY 11th

Now Italy has declared war. As Mr. Head said it was no surprise, that Mussolini looks a nasty piece of work if ever I saw one. George said whenever he sees him on the newsreel he thinks how stupid he looks strutting about in that silly uniform. The tomato plants are doing well, I had to tie them up again this afternoon. Mrs. Wentworth said that she had a recipe book, an old one that tells how to preserve tomatoes by drying them. She is going to copy it out for me so I can try it if I do not have enough preserving jars this year, although Freddie said he thinks he knows where he may be able to get hold of some down Bury way.

IS YOUR JOURNEY REALLY NECESSARY?

RAILWAY EXECUTIVE COMMITTEE

CONSERVE FUEL, WALK!

WEDNESDAY 12th

Jack said that George has asked him if he would like to go to Newmarket tonight to see Eric Boon box at the Memorial Hall. I don't think they will be able to go because Jack has hardly enough petrol for his round as it is, and George is no better off at the moment, which is a shame because he used to know Eric Boon. Young Freddie Walton asked me if I would like to make a bet on the Derby. I told him I don't agree with him taking bets because if he gets caught he will be in trouble.

THURSDAY 13th

I did some cooking and baking for Mrs. Wentworth today and she gave me the recipe for drying tomatoes. She also showed me some newspaper cuttings about the ministry asking us to eat more herrings to save them being wasted. I told her that most people I know would eat as many herrings and kippers as they could get hold of. It is nice to know that there is something we are not going to go short of. Cut half a dozen lettuces and some good size cabbages from the garden today and took some to Mr. Head. He likes his cabbage steamed until just tender and to eat it with melted butter. One of the doctors who treated him in France told him to eat it like that and he thinks that it helps to keep colds away. I have never known him to have a bad one.

FRIDAY 14th

Terrible news, no church bells from this Sunday, it won't be the same. Things are sounding bad for those poor people in Paris. It says in the paper that our boys dropped 1,000 bombs on Jerry last night, from the French coast to the northern approaches of Paris. George at the pub said he couldn't pick up Bremen and Hamburg on the wireless last night and thinks that there must have been a raid on the night before. I hope Bobby 'B' is alright. Johnny 'G' and two of his friends from SM (*Swanton Morley*) are coming on Sunday for their dinner if they can.

SATURDAY 15th

I have just been told that Johnny 'C' has been posted. George at the pub said that he thinks it is something to do with the big night raids on the Ruhr a few nights ago.

SUNDAY 16th

As I had nobody over today, after church and seeing to Mr. Head, Mavis and I went for a picnic by the river. It was a lovely day and the river was so nice and cool we sat on the bank with our feet in the water. We used the picnic hamper that Alfred bought me for Christmas all those years ago; it still has all its crockery and things. We had cold chicken, pickles and some of Mavis's bread. She is turning into a really good little bread-maker. Freddie came wandering along about one o'clock, whistling away with his hands in his pockets without a care in the world. He looked like someone from before the war. We had plenty of food so he had a good old tuck in. He said he is thinking of joining the LDVs (later known as the Home Guard) but had not made his mind up yet as he needed his evenings free. We came home just after four. Doris wants me to put in a couple of days in the shop this week as she has to go to see a friend who is staying in Ipswich at the White Horse.

MONDAY 17th

Everyone who came in the shop was shocked about Paris. Mavis is worried because if you look at the map in the paper it looks as if the Germans are nearly here. I told her that taking Paris is a lot different from taking London. The Germans bit off more than they could chew when they declared war on us and that they will not get across the channel. She cheered up a bit after that. We must not let the war get us down. If we do then the Germans are winning before they even get here. If they knew what was waiting to have a go at them over here they would not dare to try. The King has said that we shall never turn back. Registered for margarine today.

WEDNESDAY 19th

Did not get much sleep last night as there was a warning sounded. It said in George's paper that there was a raid over the Thames. It also said that we hit ten big targets on Monday. I know of Hamburg and Cologne but some of the other places I do not. I must get a book out of the library so I know more about what's going on. Says there was smoke over 2,000 feet in the air. They mention some night raiders attacking the marshalling yards at a place called Hamm. It makes me worry about Stanley working at Clapham. I hope he keeps a look out for the bombs when he's fire-watching. He's too old for all that really; he did his bit in the last lot. Mavis Emery brought me some lovely strawberries for jam. I'll make some scones for my boys for Sunday tea. Frank popped in to say cheerio, he's moving on. He didn't say where but he looked very pale. I think he's frightened poor boy, and doesn't want to show it. Just think, last year all this hadn't started.

A **LONDONER'S VIEW** OF THE AIR – THE VAPOUR TRAILS MARK THE TWISTING TURNS OF THE COMBATANTS. JUNE 1940

THURSDAY 20th

I had a little parcel today from Glim. She has started work in a dress shop in the West End and sent me a pair of lovely kid gloves and some signed photographs of Max Miller, Ben Lyon and Bebe Daniels. She went to a show a few weeks ago and as she knows the stage manager she was able to go backstage. She knows how much Stanley likes Max Miller and said that she would like me to send it to him for his birthday. I have put Ben and Bebe in my album with my other theatrical bits and pieces. I wish I had kept all my programmes, they were happy times for Alfred and me. He did like the Music Hall so. He used to say that nothing makes your step lighter than a good laugh. Stanley used to say that Alfred looked like Max Miller about the eyes, sort of cheeky. I could never see it myself, but he could certainly be cheeky sometimes.

FRIDAY 21st

I had a days work at the tea shop in town today, only until early afternoon. Afterwards I met up with Mavis to go and visit Edna Washbrook. We have not seen her since April and her Ted is at home. He was wounded just before Dunkirk and came back with the rest of them. He told us what it was like on the beaches. He said that the worst thing for him was the terrible smell. He had spent most of the time when he was waiting for a boat in a shell hole on the beach and had been shot at by German planes more than once. He doesn't remember getting on the boat or anything of the crossing and he says he is grateful for that, as he missed some of the worst parts he thinks. He says he will never forgive the Belgian King Leopold for what he did and neither will most of the Belgian people. Ted said that they were as brave as the next man and deserved a better king. It was nothing short of treachery to capitulate while they (*the British Expeditionary Forces*) were in such a bad position with their backs to the sea and no obvious way out. Ted called him some names I can tell you. He says that one of the men in hospital with him kept talking about someone with a little boat called Shamrock who was one of the bravest men there and not even in uniform. He took no end of men from the beaches to the big ships and he should be decorated for what he did as well as the others who turned up to help. Ted said that he is much better now but has been told it is unlikely he will be A1 and is likely to be invalided out. I told him that if he ever feels like it I am sure he could be a great help with the LDVs. Edna told us as we were leaving that in a way she is glad Ted was wounded as at least he got back in one piece.

SATURDAY 22nd

Mr. Head came round for supper and to listen to the wireless for an hour or two. We sat in the garden with the window open and drank some of the port I had in the pantry I was saving. Two of the boys from Coltishall came round for a beer or two and fell asleep on the grass.

MONDAY 24th

Jack brought me several bags of beans for preserving. I have to get more salt for drying. Nothing must be wasted this year as winter could be hard and I do not wish to be caught out like I was last January. Frank sent me a lovely brooch as a leaving present. A picture of a cat, just like Albert only not quite so fat. Young Freddie Walton offered me some whisky this evening when he brought the preserving jars he promised. There are boxes and boxes of them and all new by the look of them. He said that he exchanged them for some wire netting and fence posts with someone in Lynn. He said I should be careful as some are cracked and have missing lids. I bought a bottle of the whisky as it is in a good cause. He said he would not take anything for the jars other than the odd full one when he needs it. I know a lot of people say he should be in uniform him not being reserved or ill or anything, but he is a nice boy and people should not be so quick to say such things about him. He is a very helpful boy and not a shirker as some say. He works very hard for the old folk and does the work that a lot of the men folk would do if they were here. He does his bit. Mr. Head would have to do without his bedtime tot if not for Freddie making sure he always had a bottle in his sideboard.

ALWAYS READY TO GO...

TUESDAY 25th

Spent the day helping Mavis picking tomatoes round at Jack's and then at the pub. George has done very well with his this year and we picked some of them green for chutney. Mavis is helping me out with the bottling and preserving this year as I am fair run off my feet at the moment what with the beans and everything.

UNDATED

I was at the hall this evening to get the tea ready for the platoon and while I was there Gordon Housego showed me his Picture Post and it really upset me. It was all about what to do if the Germans invade and there was a picture of one of their tanks coming down one of our village streets. Gordon kept saying this is what to do when we are invaded as if they were sure to. I told him to put his book away and not show it to anyone else. I told him he was not talking like someone in uniform should do. He went quite red but I was angry. If poor Mavis or Mr. Head saw that book I do not know what they would do. When one of the Blythe boys, who was home on leave, came over for tea last week he was talking about how important morale is. He said that when the news they got was good everyone seemed to do their jobs much better, and when it was bad everything went wrong. His brother Will is in Catterick same as he is.

GET A HOBBY! SOMETHING TO TAKE YOUR MIND OFF THINGS?

July 1940

During the long hot summer of 1940 the first bombs fell on Norwich. The Battle for Britain began.

TUESDAY 2nd

Up early this morning to enjoy the garden. The sweet peas are the best I have seen and are like a colourful curtain across the garden. I must be sure to cut them back soon to get a second show and the same with the Virginian Stock. I cut off the dead blooms from the roses like Jack said. Mavis has done a good job tying up the hollyhocks, I lost most of them last year by not doing them before the wind got them. Young Freddie is taking Fred to Brandon to sell his rabbit skins, he says it will keep him in beer for the rest of the year.

TUESDAY 9th

It is hard to take in, it really is. I know people from the city who have never believed they would ever be bombed and said that all the precautions, shelters and things are a waste of money. Mrs. Wentworth has always said that any factories anywhere are likely to be targets for the Germans.

(NB. Norwich was bombed on July 9th 1940 – the first of many raids.)

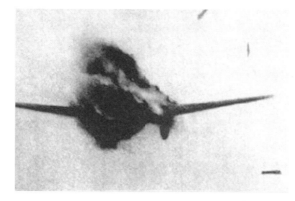

DEADLY SKIES
AN ATTACKER'S GUN
CAMERA RECORDS THE
DISINTEGRATION OF A
GERMAN HEINKEL I I I
BOMBER

SUNDAY 14th

I don't know. Mr. Churchill said in his broadcast tonight that this will be a long and hard war. I think most of us have worked that one out for ourselves. He talked about having to fight street by street if we are invaded. Rubbish. We won't be invaded. If Hitler was going to invade he would have done it when we were not expecting it, when we were not looking, when our backs were turned, like cowards always do. Well, our backs are not turned and he knows it so he won't be invading this year, next year or the year after. Now I'm going to have a good night's sleep. I have a busy day in the garden.

BE PREPARED!

MONDAY 15th

Picked a fine load of peas today. I sold some of them in the shop.

WEDNESDAY 24th

The LDVs are now called the Home Guard. Why they didn't call them that in the first place I don't know, it sounds much better.

FRIDAY 26th

John 'H' and Harry (*ground crew from Swanton Morley*) came round for a bite to eat this evening. We had our supper in the garden. Harry said that the Battle for Britain was turning out to be just that. He told me how some of our pilots are surprised about how easy some of the German fighters are to shoot down. They say it's just like they think our boys aren't as good as they are. Which is a mistake as far as they are concerned, and long may they continue to make it.

ATTENTION!
A PROUD HOME GUARD
INSPECTED BY CHURCHILL

August 1940

This was the month that Germany declared a total blockade of Britain and the Luftwaffe were ordered to 'overcome the RAF, with all means at its disposal'. Thus clearing the skies over the channel for Operation Sealion – the invasion of Britain.

SATURDAY 3rd

I knew we should not think that the Germans had given up the invasion yet. And now Mr. Churchill says so too. If we start thinking that Jerry can't do it he will just because we stop looking out.

SUNDAY 4th

It was too hot to do very much today, so I just went to church, cooked Mr. Head his lunch, baked some bread and spent the rest of the day in the garden reading. Beryl popped round for a cup of tea and said that she wished she had started a diary when war broke out. I didn't tell her I was keeping one, I have not told anyone. Mrs. Wentworth told me that servicemen are told not to keep any sort of diary just in case someone who shouldn't gets to see it. Just to be on the safe side I shall keep mine under the boards in the bottom of the wardrobe with my other bits and bobs. Albert only got off his barrel to have his dinner today, he loves the sun. I may go to Norwich market with Jack on Thursday.

AN **RAF CREW** WAITING FOR ACTION – AUGUST 1940

MONDAY 5th

I was up early this morning, and had my morning cup of tea in the garden. The air was lovely and cool, just a little breeze blowing across the fields. I had a couple of hours at Mrs. Wentworth's this morning making sandwiches for the meeting this afternoon; she paid me even though there was no need. She told us about some of the places that we have been giving a pasting in Germany.

UNDATED

There was a lot on the news tonight about the air attacks. Over seventy Germans were shot down and not many of ours, although one is too many. Jack said tonight as we were listening that he thought this was it, if Jerry breaks through now we are in trouble, this really is the Battle of Britain. Mrs. Wentworth says her husband calls it the Battle for Britain. But there is a spirit in the air, a sort of a feeling about at the moment that seems to tell us that he won't.

THURSDAY 15th

I saw Fred Barnard shooting sparrows today. He said the Ministry of Agriculture has told every one to kill as many as they can. Poor little things. Mavis told me that her Andy has been posted abroad. She got a letter this morning. He was supposed to get leave at the end of the month. I'm going to ask her to help me with the rooms at the pub to take her mind off things.

THE LACK OF PLANES WAS THE MESSAGE BEHIND THIS POSTER **INCREASE PRODUCTIVITY!**

FRIDAY 16th

The front page of the Mirror says our boys shot down 144 out of 1,000 yesterday and it was the greatest day of air attacks in the war. We lost 27 planes and nineteen pilots. Poor brave boys, and boys is what most of them are. It also says that the aerodrome at Croydon has suffered a raid. Aerodromes in the north and south, it says, were hit as well. I read this story to Mr. Head:

'The Germans fired at our boys all the time, but it seemed that the RAF pilots were holding their fire and trying to turn them off by sheer daring. They flew within inches of them. Time after time I thought the RAF men were going to ram the bombers, but they swept past them. The Germans had had enough. They fled to the coast, and as they got into the distance, over sparsely populated country, the RAF men went for them hell for leather.'

It cheered him up no end. I will keep this cutting. There is a little bit in there too about the Duke and Duchess of Windsor on their way to the Bahamas. He says that they need a rest after their experiences in France. It is alright for some. I expect some of our boys could do with a rest in the sun. And to think he was our King. It's a good job he isn't now that's a fact. The one we have now is a proper King doing a good job and so is the Queen. They are a credit to our country. Doris asked for an extra two dozen scones for tomorrow. Two guests at the pub until Sunday teatime. They will be out for meals so it's not too much work.

SUNDAY 25th

Jack told me that they had a regular at the hall today going through a few things. He said he was quite impressed by how well they drilled. Although I don't say that much about it to anyone else it worries me when I read about just how many German planes get through to this country. Mrs. Wentworth told me after church today that it was inevitable that Hitler would start on our major cities before too long, and would get a very nasty shock when he does. I don't like the thought of Stanley being so near to the railway yards (*Clapham*) if anything like that does start. I think I'll ask him to come and stay here for a while.

MONDAY 26th

Edna heard from her aunt. She was away when the attack came. So there's a worry gone. All the boys who came on Tuesday seemed extra nervous. There was a young Flight Lieutenant, a friend of Frank, who told me that some nights he is afraid to go to sleep because of the dreams he has. He looked as though he hadn't had much sleep. We sat in the garden on our own and drank some of the Haig whisky my Stanley sent me to save for Christmas. I'm sure he won't mind. The poor boy is so worried it did him good to talk. He told me he just didn't want to die. He was very drunk when he left. I told them they had to look out for each other and they'd all be alright. They're all coming for steak and kidney pudding on Friday. Albert is sleeping outside on top of his barrel as it is a warm night.

TUESDAY 27th

Ted gave me some fish heads and bones for Albert. The Vicar came round the other day for a cup of tea and told me he thought Albert was too fat to be healthy. I told him to stick to his job and leave looking after Albert to me, as he is a happy cat which is more than can be said for some of his parishioners. Did some baking for Mrs. Wentworth this morning and she remarked how good the harvest was this year. Everything seems to be in abundance, apples and everything. What with that and the RAF doing so well she said that she had a feeling the tide was turning in our favour. Went with Jack to the Standard (Dereham) for a drink and to call on Beryl at the boarding house. As she is on her own now she asked Jack if he could repair a broken banister on her landing, as one of her paying guests nearly had a nasty fall on his way to bed last week.

WEDNESDAY 28th

Jack brought me six pigeons. I'll cook them for Sunday supper. It may be the last time some of the boys will be able to get over for a while. I am expecting several new boys as I hear there have been quite a few extra ground crew brought in with lorry loads of spare parts. Stanley said in his letter today that there was a story in the paper about a German raider who dropped a bomb over the channel straight into the funnel of a trawler and that the skipper picked it up, ran onto the deck and threw it overboard. Stanley said he found it hard to believe and so do I.

THURSDAY 29th

One of the 'boys', John 'S' came round late tonight on his way back to Coltishall. He gave me a letter from Ian 'R'. It was the first time I had seen him for days and he looked strained and very weary. He told me that things had not been good in the last few days and that Jerry had been throwing everything at them and done terrible damage to our airfields down south, but had been sent packing. He told me that he knew now that we would win the war without any doubt at all. He said that we will break Jerry before Christmas as he just does not have what it takes to win. I am glad he told me that as even though on the news today it says that we shot down nearly thirty German planes today it is a worry when there is so much fighting going on over this country. Stanley has asked me to go and stay with him for a few days, I've written to tell him that I will go next week if I can. Jack said that he heard there is an instructor from the Army coming again this week to see how the platoon is getting on.

FRIDAY 30th

I spent the morning in the garden. It is all I can do to keep everything watered. How we all wish it would rain. I can't remember when we last had a good downpour. Went into Watton today with Jack and stopped off to see Edna Brice. She has recovered from her chest infection and is looking very chipper and bustling around as good as ever, she puts me to shame with the amount of work she does. There is a huge pile of socks she has knitted for the lads and she still finds time to help out with the refugees next door. Her grandson Bob is coming home sometime next month, she hopes, as he is being posted. She tells me she had a lovely seventy-third birthday party. She was born the same year as Queen Mary.

A **HURRICANE**
PILOT GIVING
THE THUMBS-UP

September 1940

The month that saw the start of the Blitz, Hitler's ambitions thwarted by 'the Few' – and Betty going to Clapham to see her half-brother Stanley – with the ulterior motive of bringing him back to the relative safety of Norfolk.

SUNDAY 1st

Went to church. Mrs. Wentworth wasn't there as she has some ministry people staying for the weekend. I went over to give her a hand with cooking supper for them. I had five boys over from Coltishall with Mavis, Mr. Head and Freddie. One of the young engineers, Charlie, cheered us all up no end today. He brought his banjo and sang us some very funny songs. They were a bit on the rude side some of them but I've heard worse on the halls. I was telling them about Max Miller and some of the things he used to sing. I'd love to see one of his shows again. I had a drink with him once when some friends and I met him in a pub after a show. I think it was in Kilburn but I can't be sure. I have been in so many pubs after shows in my time it's hard to remember. He seemed a very kind and polite man to me. Every inch the gentleman. I remember he was wearing a very thick camel coat belted up against the weather.

MONDAY 2nd

At the meeting this afternoon Mrs. Wentworth said that she intended to have it out with her MP about the servicemen's extra 6d being delayed by four weeks when civil servants were not. As she said, this war will change a lot of things and it is up to all of us to make sure that those changes are more fair than before. Those that fight for the freedom of us all, however humble and poor they may have been before the war, deserve only the best when it is all over. I don't think any of us have ever seen her so angry about anything, not even when the temporary vicar looked straight at her and preached about a camel being more likely to go through the eye of a needle than a rich man entering the Kingdom of Heaven.

TUESDAY 3rd

Jock Naylor (local fishmonger) asked if I would help him out in the shop as his boy has to go for a medical. I said I would as he pays well and is generous with his fish. If I can get some cod I will make fish cakes for Saturday supper as Emily is coming round for the evening.

WEDNESDAY 4th

I wish I had thought about it sooner but I have been so busy. The purchase tax has come in and that means if I buy a new coat for the winter it will cost me more than it need. Never mind, I shall just have to hope for a little extra work to make up.

THURSDAY 5th

Heard today that Billy 'I' was shot down over North Weald. Poor lad. Jimmy said that it was one of the worst days of the war so far. I didn't know that his girlfriend had been killed when they bombed her airfield at the end of last month. What a terrible waste. Spent the day getting ready to go to Stanley's tomorrow. Mavis is going to stay here on the odd day to see after Albert. I told her not to spoil him but I expect that she will.

From Clapham

During her time in Clapham Betty's diary entries were not precisely dated, probably because the pace of life was rather different, and dangerous, from that which she had become accustomed in Norfolk. However, Betty appeared to be no stranger to city life; on her various visits she seemed to be quite at home in the more densely populated areas of the country. The entries that follow are, as far as can be determined, in the correct order; in brackets are the events to which it is believed Betty refers and the dates are as accurate as possible.

UNDATED

I would never have believed I would ever witness the things I have these last two days. The whole city looked as if it was on fire. Stanley said that the fires would be a target for the bombers, as everything was lit up like day. The docks look as if they caught it the worst. Stanley thinks that Jerry uses the Thames as a guide for the bombs. We spent last night trapped in a pub because the AFS (*Auxiliary Fire Service*) said that the buildings in the surrounding streets were burning badly and though it was not safe to stay where we were it was better than trying to get out. So there we stayed. We saw the AFS men going to what looked like the heart of the fires. They are some of the bravest of men in this war and that's a fact. There was a young soldier in the pub with us who had been in Portsmouth during the big raid (*mid-August*) and he said that he came up to London to see his girl for a bit of peace and quiet. The landlord told him that if anyone had told him to come to London for his nerves he had been misinformed. This raised the biggest laugh of the night. We eventually got back to Stanley's place late this afternoon. I made a good old pot full of beef stew and Norfolk dumplings and admit to having more than my share of Stanley's port so I expect to make up for my lost sleep tonight.

LONDON'S BURNING, **'THE BLITZ'**. SUMMER 1940

UNDATED

Last night, or it could have been the night before last, I really can't be sure, was a terrible thing indeed. Jack and I were caught out late and the bus we were on stopped and we had to run for a shelter while the bombs were dropping. We made it to a shelter but during the night there was a hit very close by and some said it would be better to find somewhere else but we stayed put. When we came out after the all clear it was a terrible sight. As we walked along all we could see was firemen, police and ordinary folk climbing over the bricks and broken glass looking for anyone trapped. Stanley and I tried to give a hand but we were just too tired, we seem to have walked miles. There was so much broken glass. More broken glass than anything else and those that were searching were getting badly cut. I don't know what time we got back, we just had a tot of whiskey and went to bed. I must have slept for more than twelve hours. I have just been reading the Daily Express and there is a story by one of the reporters about how she was caught out in a raid. I will keep it as it explains just what it is like. It says on the front page that Churchill thinks the invasion could come within days. Well, invasion or no invasion I shall be glad to get home. Anyway, I don't believe there will be an invasion. The Germans are bullies and I have met lots of bullies in my time and none of them were brave. And they will have to be very brave to invade us.

AN ARIEL VIEW OF LONDON DURING A BOMBING RAID

During the period August 8th to 15th some of the heaviest raids of the war were inflicted on the south of England; RAF Manston in Kent was all but destroyed. It is well documented that Hitler intended to leave London well alone (not out of any sympathy for the people living there of course; he did not relish the prospect of retaliation against Berlin), but that the first bombs to fall on the capital were in fact intended for the Thames Haven oil refineries. Churchill ordered a swift response; that response was on August 25th/26th in the form of eighty plus bombers attacking Berlin. Four more British raids followed within the next few days. Thereafter, Hitler was persuaded by members of his High Command – Göering and Kesselring included – to allow an all out day and night bombing campaign against London. The object being to force the RAF to defend the skies over the capital and, they hoped, put them in a position where the German fighters could shoot them from the air. In retrospect it is easy to see why a 'mistake' by some German bombers was assumed by the British to be a change in tactics. It was a set of events that would alter the course, and conduct, of the war.

October/November 1940

This was perhaps the most terrifying part of Betty's war; one has to read between the lines to detect that what she saw appalled her tremendously. For this portion of her journal there are no specific dates given, given the circumstances one can understand why. These months in 1940 London sustained the heaviest air raids up to that point. Those who were in the capital during this time often remarked how strange it was to see Londoners scrambling over the rubble in the morning to make their way in to work; the phrase 'London can take it' wasn't just propaganda, and reflected a spirit that was in no small part responsible for the final outcome of the war. It is a matter of record that morale in the German cities was severely damaged by allied bombing. One reason for this is likely to have been because Hitler promised that not a single bomb would fall on Berlin – his promise was not kept and the Fuhrer's fallibility started to show. The British on the other hand were promised: 'blood, toil, tears and sweat', and that is exactly what was delivered. There is a lesson in there somewhere.

The bombing of London continued. There were major raids on Birmingham, Bristol, Liverpool, Southampton and on November 14 the notorious operation 'Moonlight Sonata' began; which was to devastate Coventry with nearly 400 tons of bombs – total war became a fact of life and death. It is true to say that this period was a pivotal point in Britain's history.

Meanwhile, back in Clapham, Betty made the most of her stay – bombs or no bombs.

UNDATED

Stanley tried to get in to see some of his old workmates in Notting Hill today and when he got back, very late, he said that he had been helping people to get some of their things out of the rubble of their house just off the Kings Road. He was in an awful mess as he had been at it all day. I often wonder how we manage to get anything done these days as there has been a raid every night for the last two months or more. It's a wonder anyone manages to sleep, but we do. I shall be glad to get home and I'm glad that Stanley has agreed to come with me, as I don't like to think of him being here on his own with all this going on.

UNDATED

I had a letter from Mavis today. She says that everything is alright at home and she has had several letters from her Andy. He says he can't say what he's doing or where he is but he is not exactly in the front line and is enjoying what he is doing. There is a chance that he may be able to get home on a forty-eight before Christmas. Stanley and I went to the Red Lion tonight and when Jerry came over we went into the cellar and stayed for the all-clear. Frank, the landlord, has fitted it out like home from home and it is much more comfortable than the public shelters. Most of us down there were regulars and as such we felt less nervous somehow. There was a fireman with us who had helped with the clearing up at Buckingham Palace after it was bombed (*September 1940*). He said that there was a huge bomb crater and if it had been a few feet in the other direction there could have been people killed. The landlord said as we were leaving that if we wanted to stay down here on other nights instead of using one of the public shelters we would be more than welcome and he would save us places.

THE LONDONER'S SHELTER **THE UNDERGROUND PLATFORM**

UNDATED

As I was going to get the paper this morning I heard a noise like the end of the world had come. The whole side of a bombed house completely collapsed just as I passed it. Something knocked me down but apart from being covered in dust from head to foot I am alright. A kind constable walked me home and I made him a cup of tea. He told me about a raid he was in a few weeks ago when he had had a narrow squeak. A great big dollop of hot lead from the lead roof of an old building had just missed him, but had scorched his uniform. As he said "you don't expect a roof to melt and nearly send you to your maker or houses to fall down as you walk along the street".

UNDATED

Everyone I have seen today is talking about Coventry. According to the news and the papers it is one of the worst things to happen so far. I think this has affected morale here in London even more than the raids here. I suppose as they can't see what has happened they fear the worst. Stanley and I are spending the night at Frank's pub. We are taking some cards and have promised to teach some of the others how to play canasta. Stanley says he is sure they would rather have a game of whist but I think something a bit more difficult will help to take people's mind of things a little.

TUESDAY 19th

Spent the day cleaning the house and getting everything ship-shape. I have cooked Stanley's main meal so all he has to do is heat it through. I am going to visit some of the winter sales tomorrow. Mavis and Doris have given me a shopping list for all sorts of things: sheets, pyjamas, tablecloths, and Mr. Head needs quite a few things, they will do as early Christmas presents. How I shall carry it all I just don't know. Stanley showed me a story in the paper that farm workers and farmers in the army can have leave of 28 days if needs be. Perhaps Jim Savage can get home to help out now that his dad is laid up with his broken leg. I must send the cutting to Marjorie is case she hasn't heard. I heard on the wireless that the Dunlop factory in Coventry was badly bombed. That was where Kenneth Rhodes worked before he joined up.

WEDNESDAY 20th

I've written to Mavis to tell her that I managed to get most of the things she wanted from a shop near Victoria Station. I wish I had had the money to buy more because I am not sure if there will be much around this time next year. I bought three cycle capes, one for Jack as his is getting beyond repair, one for young Freddie and one for Fred. I shall give them theirs for Christmas. I would have had a job carrying everything but I went to visit Glim and she came shopping with me. She has a new job in one of the big stores in Kensington and starts next week, it's only until the end of January but it is better than nothing. We got back just before black-out and Stanley was already home. He'd been out helping some people to clear up. I cooked fish and chips as Glim managed to get some lovely plaice. It was nearly 3/- a pound and she insisted on paying. We are all spending the night in Frank's cellar. Glim is having a rare old time singing requests, her voice is as good as ever, she should be on the wireless as she is better than some that are.

THURSDAY 21st

We are in the middle of packing so we stayed in tonight to get it all finished. We will say our goodbyes to Frank and everyone at the pub in the morning. Frank and his family have been very kind to Stanley and to me while I have been here and I am going to give him the rechargeable lamp that Jack bought me for Christmas last year. Frank's need here in the black-out is greater than mine back home. I'm sure Jack wouldn't mind. And it will give me more room to take back all the things I have bought. Stanley is using his big sea trunk. I don't know what train we will be catching yet.

Back home in Norfolk

UNDATED

We are just about straight after getting back. Albert gave me an old-fashioned look. I gave him some of the fish Mavis had left for him and he fell asleep on his chair. I don't think I would like to live in a city again while this war is on. I didn't realise how much it gets on your nerves having to go into a shelter every night. Stanley says that he finds it difficult to get to sleep it being so quiet, but he'll soon get used to it. I told him that all that dust can't have been any good for his chest and I'm sure he'll feel better in himself after a few weeks in the country and he won't want to go back to London. I had a letter from Margaret Black in Coventry, she has been living in Derby for the last three years and was back in Coventry to visit her old school. She wrote to tell me that the shop where I used to work was hit during the raids. That is so sad because it was a nice little place and holds some pleasant memories for me.

WEDNESDAY 27th

I have spent the day at Mrs. Wentworth's sorting out clothes for parcels. There is a lorry picking them up sometime before Christmas but we don't know exactly when so we thought we had better get them ready just in case. There was a nice mackintosh there that would fit Mr. Head and he needs a new one badly. I asked Mrs. Wentworth if it would be alright if I took it and replaced it with one of Stanley's which he doesn't wear because he says it isn't long enough to keep his legs dry, and she said I could. I will take it round to Mr. Head in the morning. At the pub tonight young Freddie asked me if we would be having a Christmas party again this year so I asked George if anything had been planned while I was away. He said that everyone who wanted to come for Christmas dinner was welcome, so I said I would help with everything same as last year.

THURSDAY 28th

Stanley has been hard at it today fixing the hinge on my bedroom window and tidying up the garden. It was so foggy this morning it was difficult to find my way down the garden to get the wood in; it's because I am so low and it rolls in off the fields. It didn't lift until well past eleven this morning and came down again in the afternoon. Jack bought me another lamp to replace the one I gave to Frank. I told him to think of it as my Christmas present for this year as they are very expensive, but very welcome just the same. Doris asked Mavis to ask me to make her up a special order of drop scones for Saturday and she will let me have the flour etc. tomorrow. I will be busy tomorrow because as well as the usual baking for the shop I am making the LDV's soup for the weekend, and they will need extra as another platoon is coming over for a meeting and they will need feeding with something warm if the weather is as damp as it is today. Freddie asked me if I would like two pullets for 5/- each, he's bringing them round tomorrow. I could use some extra eggs with Stanley here.

A RECRUITMENT POSTER FOR THE **WOMEN'S LAND ARMY**

FRIDAY 29th

Doris heard that some people are getting more than their fair share from Fred Hipwell. One of her customers was at the Knox's today and there was a great number of packages of meat going in through the back door and they were not best pleased that he had seen what was going on. George said that they had tried to persuade him to sell some of his stock and he told them where to get off. As he said this is not the time to take advantage of having a few bob, and he wouldn't even serve them now if they came in for a drink. Not that they would want to rub shoulders with the likes of ordinary folk. Fred Barnard and Jack are going to the Bull at Watton tomorrow night and Mavis, Doris and I are spending the day at Gilbert and Marjorie's. They have very kindly offered us some of their bottled fruit and tomatoes. They have some that is a few years old but they tried it and it is still alright. They need to clear out one of their store-rooms for two land army girls they are having and they would like us to take some of the bottled stuff and hand it round to anyone who is short. Mavis is going to put some of it in her back parlour cupboard and the rest George has said we can keep in the big cupboard where he keeps the Christmas bits and pieces.

SATURDAY 30th

We have moved all the jars from Marjorie's. There was a real old selection. Plums that her mother had bottled in 1933, raspberries, jars and jars of jam and chutney, damson jam, bottled cherries, rhubarb jam, blackberry jam and bottled blackberries, apple chutney, bottled tomatoes and a dozen jars of marmalade. There is a great deal we will be able to do with all that. I have a recipe for pheasant and cherries and one for pheasant and blackberries that will do for rabbit as well. George kindly drove it all back for us. I'm very ready for bed after today.

December 1940

Betty prepared for the second Christmas of the war.

TUESDAY 3rd

It was a bit raw this morning so I banked the fire up well before we went to bed tonight. Did some shopping in Watton for Mr. Head, and got a lift home with Jack. We gave a lift to some airmen who were off on leave. One of them looked just like Ted Sturgess's brother Brian only younger. He is a mechanic from Arbroath, only nineteen. He has tried to get leave to go home for Hogmanay but couldn't. I told him if he wanted to he could come over with his mates for New Year either to the pub or to mine. They make a big thing of New Year the Scottish, same as we do Christmas. There was a lot of coming and going on the way back from Watton. We saw at least ten lorries in a row. Must be something going on. George told us tonight that someone was seen trying to break into the hen house up at the big house last night. It was only the dogs barking that made the gardener go and take a look. He found the door half forced open and saw a van turning out of the drive. Like Freddie said, chickens are valuable things these days and I had better keep an eye on mine. I'd find it hard to get hold of good layers like them at the moment. Fred Barnard said he has got a rough idea he saw the same van poking about when he was out with his gun the other night, he didn't see who it was as they were too far away, but they were driving past the long field up near Jenkins hollow, just past the old pit, and turned off up towards the old barns.

WEDNESDAY 4th

On the way back from Marjorie's tonight Mavis and I saw a van, it was
like the one Jack used to drive before he had the Morris, going down the
back road towards the old farm track that leads to one-armed Bob's old
cottage, and you would not get a van through there. We waited for a few
minutes and we couldn't hear anything so we came home. I don't like
to think of strangers driving around here late at night. I told Jack and he
said he would take a look down that way tomorrow and see what's what.

THURSDAY 5th

Ted Sturgess came into the shop today to ask where he could find Jack.
He told me that Harry Shaw had had twelve chickens stolen and that
he thought they had been taken by the same people who had been seen
poking around lately. I had better make sure I keep an eye on mine. At
the meeting at Mrs. Wentworth's this afternoon she was telling us about
the restrictions on the supply of luxury goods like knitted clothes, gloves
and the like. She was not pleased about how this would be controlled
as they were not to be rationed but as it was being planned the people
with the most money would get more than their fair share. She has written
a letter to Captain Lyttleton (President of the Board of Trade) about it
and asking him to reconsider his plans. We were all asked if we would
like to add anything. Freddie came round just after half-past ten tonight
with some things he wants me to look after for Christmas. There are
two big boxes full. He says there are some bottles and tins and some
Will's Whiffs he managed to get hold of in Thetford. I told him how the
smell of a cigar always reminds me of Christmas.

FRIDAY 6th

Had a letter from Glim. She asked me if I had heard Star Time with
Evelyn Laye on the wireless a few days ago, she had missed it and wanted
to know what it was like. I wish I had. I went with my Alfred to see her
in Waltz Time in '33. We ate fish and chips on the way back to our digs
as it was after nine o'clock and the landlady didn't serve food or allow

us to take any back after that time. It rained and we had to shelter in Woolworth's doorway until it eased off and then we ran home under Alfred's mac. Good order from the shop this week including some Christmas puddings, small ones for presents to send away. Stanley has taken quite a shine to looking after the chickens. He takes his mug of tea in the morning into the chicken house to sit with them. He says that the reason they have been laying so well lately is because he talks to them. Maybe he is right. Freddie came round with the chicken feed and he had some shepherd's pie with us.

SATURDAY 7th

Stanley and I delivered the baking to the shop and then went into Dereham with George. I had to pick up some bits and pieces for Mrs. Wentworth from Kingston as she is laid up with a bad cold at the moment and Mr. Wentworth is home this afternoon with some of the people he works with. They are staying overnight. Navel types I think she said. George asked us tonight if we would like to spend Christmas day at the pub, the same as last year. Jack and I said we would and as Mavis's Andy has not been able, again, to get leave I am sure she would like to. Mr. Head said he would and thought it would be a good idea to invite some of the boys from 'C' (*RAF Coltishall*) and 'SM' (*RAF Swanton Morley*). It would at least help to take their minds off them being away from home. Beryl suggested that if we had some chickens and pheasants on the go, as well as the turkey, we would be able to give them a meal if they were not able to make it for when we had ours. Jack said that Bob Webster, who is in his platoon, would be on his own this Christmas and he would like to invite him too. It looks as if we will have even more round the table than last year. We have no bookings for the rooms over Christmas which surprises me. Doris says that she thinks Edna Bailey's boy may want one as he is coming over this Christmas and what with Edna's mother-in-law coming as well they will be short of room. Stanley had a letter from his neighbour in Clapham to let him know his house was alright and that he was lighting a fire in the stove once a week to keep the place aired.

MONDAY 9th

Fred came round just after eight this morning to ask me about how to make a hay-box. He has had several enquiries in the last few weeks. I told him that when my mother used to use one it was about three feet by three feet by two feet. She used to leave our porridge in it to finish cooking overnight in one covered pot and the stew in the other. The porridge used to do most of its cooking overnight and only needed a bit of extra cooking to heat it up in the morning, as did the stew. I told Fred that it needed to be able to hold two good sized cooking pots with plenty of fine, clean, hay packed into the bottom of the box and around the sides. Leaving holes like nests to hold the pots. With hay filled pillows to lay over the top of them and a tight fitting lid to the box. I told him that I would be happy to make the pillows in return for one of the finished boxes. He says that he will be able to sell them for about seven and six each. They are a good idea now that fuel is likely to be in short supply. Jennifer Medwin came round with Mavis and I asked her what she was doing for Christmas as she would be more than welcome to spend it with the rest of us at the pub if she wanted to. She said she would see what Mr. Dobbs said. She did not want to offend them but she said she would like to get away from the farm for Christmas if she could, and she knew that they were having family to stay and they may need her bed but not like to say.

TUESDAY 10th

Had a couple of hours working at Mrs. Wentworth's. She told me that London was attacked quite badly last night. After lunch was cleared away we went to the school to see the headmistress about the children who were to stay at the Wentworth's over the Christmas holiday. As we walked towards the door we could hear the children singing 'Away in a Manger'. It took me back I can tell you. Miss Dobson said that there are five who need somewhere to stay over Christmas, two boys and three girls. All under eight. Miss Dobson asked me if I would like to join her sewing circle making clothes for the needy, I told her that much though

I would like to help, I had spent years and years going round the country making and repairing theatrical costumes and I promised myself after that I would only do the barest little of sewing I could get away with. I will cook and bake until the cows come home but not sew. She laughed and said that she was sure she would be the same. I promised to ask Mavis as she is very nifty with a needle and thread. We had a guided tour of the school and saw all the Christmas decorations the children had made. Mrs. Wentworth said on the way back that she would ask the children staying with her to help decorate her house, that way they would feel more at home. It made me feel quite full of the Christmas spirit. It was getting quite dark by the time I got back home.

FRIDAY 13th

News came through today that we have taken Sidi Barrani from the Italians which is good news. Maude Scott's boy Wesley is in North Africa. I remember her telling me that he told her that sometimes all he could see is red and yellow sand and not a bit of green anywhere. Must seem odd for a country boy. Did my baking early today and dropped off Doris's order just after four o'clock. I have made some pies and tarts for the pub and Mavis is seeing to looking after the guests over the weekend as I have a special cooking job to do at the Wentworth's.

SATURDAY 14th

Staying overnight at the Wentworth's as there is quite a lot to do. There are a lot of people staying and there are cars parked everywhere. People who work with Mr. Wentworth and their drivers. And they all need feeding and somewhere to sleep. They all leave tomorrow afternoon. They have been locked in the drawing room all day apart from when they had dinner. I think they must have been talking about North Africa as I heard some places mentioned that have been in the paper. They have certainly got through some whisky and brandy tonight. I even had some myself with Mrs. Wentworth in her sitting room. We had finished clearing up by nine o'clock and she insisted I put my feet up for the rest of the evening. We got to talking about my time touring and she was telling me how her Grandmother used to take her to the Shepherd's Bush Empire. She has seen Max Miller, Bud Flanagan and the Crazy Gang. I told her about some of the things they used to get up to which she found very funny. I had not noticed until tonight how much Mrs. Wentworth looks like Peggy Ashcroft, only taller and with blonde hair. She is a very serious person who is very worried about what will happen after the war. She says that after the last one things changed but not all for the better. She says that she watched the Jarrow hunger marchers from the window of her dad's office and she had never forgotten the looks on their faces. She said that the same thing must not be allowed to happen again and that after this war there must be a proper fair share for everyone as they are all fighting for it. She said something else that I must remember; the whole country has fought this war and would continue to and that it seems odd to some that when our cities are bombed the people who live there still get up in the morning and make their way in to work. When she was in London during the bombing she saw bombed out shops with funny notices up saying things like: 'WE ARE OPEN FOR BUSINESS. OH BOY ARE WE OPEN FOR BUSINESS' and 'JERRY TRIED TO JUMP THE QUEUE AND CUT UP ROUGH WHEN WE WOULDN'T SERVE HIM' outside. It is because we can still live a normal life in times like these that makes the war worth winning, and our winning certain. That is what morale is all about, and is another front of the war. She says it makes us warriors all. Mr. Wentworth she told me does not hold with what she says about how things should be after the war and she says that she will change his mind for him if he won't do it for himself.

SUNDAY 15th

When I got back last night Mavis had put the Christmas decorations up, the tree that Fred had promised me and everything. It really does look a picture. This afternoon Freddie came round with some chicken food and there was a familiar face looking out of the window of the van he had borrowed. It was little Tyke. Only he has grown quite a bit since I last saw him. He is as big as a greyhound and very woolly. Freddie says that he is very attached to him and takes him out quite a bit. His owners don't mind and he says that Tyke likes to stick his head out of the window and feel the wind up his ears. And to think what could have happened to the little fellow. I told Freddie he deserves to feel proud of himself for what he did in finding him a home. I asked Freddie if there was any news about his uncle Herbert in Sheffield (*Sheffield was heavily bombed early in December 1940*). He is alright because he had moved to Carlisle in the Spring. Two staying at the pub, a young couple on leave. Mavis is doing for them.

MONDAY 16th

Freddie came round very early this morning with a rare old collection. Where he gets these things from I can't imagine. There are razor blades, scented soap and all sorts of creams and things. Freddie says he bought them from a man who bought them from a bombed out chemist. He gave me the pick of the lot for presents in return for some eggs this week, as he can trade them for some petrol which he needs for a trip down to Bury before Christmas. Jack came up with a bright idea today about how to help the Vicar with his blackout. He said that if he was to paint the edges of some of the panes with black paint it might solve the problem. He will have to do something because you can see the vicarage from miles away from a certain angle. I showed Mavis a photograph I have in my album of Peggy Ashcroft, and she said straight away that it looked like Mrs. Wentworth, they could be sisters and twins at that in the right light. Doris has given some cakes and things to the school for their Christmas party. Jack took them this afternoon. We heard what sounded like heavy bombers going over tonight, not overhead but more out towards Norwich. I wonder if they were theirs or ours. I hope we don't get any heavy raids before Christmas.

TUESDAY 17th

Spent the whole day with Mr. Head, as he has a terrible bad chest and I didn't like to leave him on his own. I enjoyed having a rest as I managed to get my feet up by his fire and feel quite refreshed for getting ready for Christmas. I shall get some present wrapping done tomorrow after I have been to help out at the school.

WEDNESDAY 18th

Had a couple of hours at Mrs. Wentworth's and the rest of the day at the school. Everyone had a rare old time. Fred made a good Father Christmas and Yo, Ho, Ho'd like Father Christmas should. Wrapped a few presents this evening – thanks to young Freddie there should be some smiling faces on Christmas morning war or no war.

HAPPY CHRISTMAS 1940

CHRISTMAS EVE

Everything is done that needs to be done for tomorrow. Mavis, Beryl, Jennifer and I had all the birds dressed and ready by three o'clock this afternoon and Jack has taken them to the pub, well the ones we will be cooking there. We will be cooking some of them here and at Mavis's to take to the pub. We have sent word out that any of 'the boys' who want to come for Christmas dinner can if they can manage it, there is plenty to go round.

BOXING NIGHT

What a Christmas. More people for Christmas dinner than I have seen for years. They were coming and going all afternoon and into the evening, just like one big happy family. Jack gave me a silver cat brooch and young Freddie gave me a lovely warm mackintosh. Very posh with a tartan lining. Jennifer said that it is just like they sell in the West End and is a very good one. Christmas does something to Mr. Head. Late on Christmas afternoon, when he had had some of George's special whisky he said that he felt like a dance. Soon so did everyone else. Mr. Head was hopping around like a two-year-old. I hadn't seen him so lively for ages. And to think a few days ago he had a bad chest. Well, I am off to bed now. I have been at Jack's for the day just having a bit of a rest before the party at the pub this evening. Just a few of us having a quiet drink and making the most of each other's company. We should not take that for granted, certainly not in war.

Here is perhaps an appropriate place to bring to a close the first part of Betty's diary, the part that documents the most devastating period of bloodshed and uncertainty man had hitherto experienced. It was the first time that war had been brought to the hearths of home by radio and the Press of the day. From that momentous Sunday of September 3rd 1939 Britain had lived through the 'phoney war', the miracle of Dunkirk, The Battle of Britain; seen the stain of Nazi tyranny knock on her very door with the fall of France, Holland and Belgium. It was a remarkable time of courage and determination. A time of heroism on an epic scale, and a time of personal courage, the kind of courage that sees a young airman climb into a cramped cockpit and go head to head with the instrument of evil hell-bent on killing in order than his evil masters could vanquish and rule.

While Betty was in Clapham in 1940 the following letter, from Ian 'R', dated September 29th 1940, was delivered by hand to her home and forwarded to her. Ian 'R' was a pilot stationed in Kent at either Hawkinge or Manston, on balance Hawkinge seems the most likely on evidence available.

Dear Betty,

I am sorry I have taken so long to put pen to paper, but things have been getting a bit hot lately as I am sure you know. I seem to have spent the last few weeks in a permanent state of readiness. I am at the moment luxuriating in a relaxed state of mind having not been required for ops for a full day. I am feeling homesick for my cockpit.

Those of us who are directly involved in the prosecution of the war fail to give enough thought to those who wait for news at home. I would like to try to put your mind at rest and that of Mr. Head. These last few weeks Germany has thrown all he has at us in these islands and we have thrown it back at him many times over. Not just those in the front line, the engineers, workers, farmers and everyone at home. Do not believe that Jerry will invade our shores because he will not. Strutting and threatening are no substitute for a belief in that for which we fight. The German soldiers and airmen, for the most part, fight because they have been told to by people they fear. They lost this war the day it started. This summer has seen the end of any chance that Hitler will fulfil his ambitions. He will not be coming after all.

Remember me to everyone. I shall see you soon.

'Oft of one wide expanse had I been told
That deep-browed Homer ruled as his demesne.
Yet did I never breathe its pure serene
Till I heard Chapman speak out loud and bold:
Then felt I like some watcher of the skies
When a new planet swims into his ken'

Ian

By Christmas 1940 it was evident that Germany could be held at bay and beaten. Victory was not seen as a certainty, however it was seen as more than possible. Betty, and people like her, were as much responsible for that victory as any.

In September 1940, somewhere in Kent, a group of youngsters enjoyed a picnic and, gazing upward, watched distant flecks weaving and diving in the clear blue sky. They knew they were watching aerial combat; they had seen several such encounters. What they would not have been aware of at the time was that they were witness to a greater battle than any fought in history, and the breaking of Hitler's ambition upon the battle-hardened axe-head of the RAF.

In those most dangerous of times, whether in the air, in some foreign land, at sea or toiling in the fields, factories, kitchens, offices and gardens on the home front, in the words of Betty's friend, Mrs. Wentworth, "We are warriors all".

Every woman not doing vital work is needed NOW

FULL INFORMATION AT THE NEAREST RECRUITING CENTRE OR YOUR EMPLOYMENT EXCHANGE

PART TWO

'Far to go and much to do'

January 1941 – September 1945

January 1941

This was the month compulsory fire-watching was introduced. By the 31st the month's civilian casualty figures were more than 3,500. In Norfolk Betty remembered a New Year of the past, and some 'paying guests' entered her life.

WEDNESDAY 1st

Here we are in 1941. A lovely New Year's night at the pub. It reminded me for some reason of a first night in Manchester in '29 I think it was. Edward Redmayne, who was putting on the show, had run out of money and it looked as if we would have to close before we opened and then at the last minute one of his old flames turned up in a great big car and saved the day. It was a big relief for all of us because we were all living hand to mouth at the time. We got through the whole run and Edward's girlfriend made a profit. That first night was one to remember. I spent today at Mrs. Wentworth's just giving her a hand with the cooking for her New Year guests. Mr. Wentworth is in London. The news of the firebomb attack came as a nasty shock and Mrs. Wentworth spent a long time on the telephone trying to find out if her husband was alright. As it turned out he was on his way to somewhere in Bedfordshire when the raid started, so much relief all round. We listened to Mr. Morrison's broadcast last night about better fire-watching as according to the papers that was why the fires got out of hand the way they did. I think it is very easy to criticise.   ·

The ferocious fire-bomb attack on December 29th 1940, came to be known as the second Great Fire of London. Many of Wren's churches were destroyed as well as the Guildhall; Samuel Johnson's house sustained serious damage.

AS THE FIRE-BOMBING INTENSIFIES MORE WOMEN ARE RECRUITED INTO THE FIRE SERVICE

THURSDAY 2nd

Jack turned his ankle while he was out with the platoon last night, running across the long field, would you believe, with the ground as hard as iron. It is no wonder he turned his ankle, he could have broken it the silly man. It has blown up like a balloon. I strapped it up as best I could and he can just about walk on it. I told him he should rest it but he says he can't as he has some deliveries to make. Stanley is going with him to give him a hand.

FRIDAY 3rd

Orders for the shop are down this week and we had to turn away a booking for the rooms at the pub as we are full up. I made some teacakes anyway, I am sure they will go. Young Freddie came round with some chicken feed. I told him I have enough for weeks but he said that it may be in short supply soon so he was stocking me up just in case. He left a half a bottle of whisky for Jack, for his ankle. Jennifer and Mavis are having a day out tomorrow in Wymondham as Mavis is going to see Mrs. Simpson from Gages about a job. Albert has spent the whole day on his chair, and only got up for his dinner. The damage done to London according to the wireless tonight is very bad. All those lovely old churches gone forever. I told Stanley that he had better leave it a while before he goes back home. Mr. Head had a letter from a friend of his in Sandgate. He is the chap that used to work at A.V. Roe that he talks about. He was the one who was making engines for airplanes in the Great War. He says he can hear all sorts flying over at night these days, theirs and ours.

SATURDAY 4th

I saw Mrs. Wentworth in the butcher's and she told me that her husband was home and that he had brought a bad cold with him. She blames it on the fact that he had spent the last few days working in a draughty old hut. Young Freddie sprang a big surprise on me today, he brought me five Runner ducks and said they are known to be very good layers. He told me to have a word with Fred about how to keep them as he is an expert about all things with fur or feather. I popped in to see him and he said that I must not let them run with the hens, so I had a word with George and he said that I can keep them in the fenced-in part of the garden at the back of the pub. There is an old hen shed that they can use as well. So Mavis and I spent the afternoon clearing the shed and settling the ducks in. Freddie said that he would drop off some meal on Monday that would help them to lay well. Fred said that they look very healthy and I would be surprised by just how many eggs they would lay. Jack's ankle is much better today and he is getting about without the stick, but he won't be out with the platoon for a few days. Stanley went pigeon shooting with Fred and was very proud to get six. It was his first time out with a gun, he'd borrowed Jack's. Pigeons in stout tomorrow. A treat for the elderly gent, a Mr. Cavendish, and his wife who are staying at the pub.

SUNDAY 5th

A bitterly cold day. Up early to get the lunch ready. Young Freddie was here just after eight with food for the ducks. He has got himself a motor-cycle and sidecar. He said that he is not always able to borrow his mates van these days. It is a Sunbeam, all shiny black and gold and he is very proud of it. He took me to church in it. What people will think I just don't know. Mr. and Mrs. Cavendish liked the pigeons in stout, as do most people. They left this afternoon and we have no bookings until Thursday. Fred came to have a look at the ducks and told me some things I didn't know. As ducks lay their eggs anywhere I have to keep them in their shed until about ten o'clock in the morning, as they usually lay before then. It is very important that they are kept in very clean conditions and fed on the right food. He said it is a good idea to feed them the odd morsel of cooked meat, but not too much and never to leave any lying around to go bad. He said that he used to feed his from his hand but you have to be careful. Fred guessed that I would see the first eggs by the end of the week when they have settled in. They are lovely birds. Jack fixed a good lock on their shed.

MONDAY 6th

Stanley went to Wymondham today to buy a pair of stout boots. He has taken to the idea of doing a bit of shooting and after he went out with Jack last week he knows he needs something better than the ones he usually wears. He managed to get a very tough pair of black boots that look as if they will last forever, but will take a lot of breaking-in. Mavis says that one of the girls in her office has joined up and that she will have to take on quite a bit of her work until they can get someone else in and train her up. One of the solicitors who she works for told her that he will be off soon so Mavis said that it will be all change by the look of it. When I look around I can see how much everything has changed in the last year and a bit. We seem to live a fairly normal life on the face of it but everything we do is affected by what we are thinking about who will leave us next, whether we will see them again, and above all when will it all end. I am sure we will win this war but what will be left of the lives we had before it started? That's the question that I ask myself the most. I know for a fact that Stanley is worried that he will not be able to get back to normal again. Apart from the time he was at sea he has spent most of his life in London and loves the place a great deal. A lot of the places he knows have gone and Lord knows how much more will go before this is all over. It will be a shame if his settled life in Clapham is over. He has some good friends there, and they are forever writing to him. Poor old Stanley. After all his time and trouble at sea all he ever wanted was a peaceful life. Perhaps he might grow to like living in the country if he can find something to occupy himself that he enjoys. I think Jack has realised what Stanley is going through and is making an effort to help him find his way. There was a good talk on the wireless tonight that I wanted to hear but I did not get home in time. I must ask Mavis if she heard it. The ducks are doing very well and eating like they have not seen food for months. Beryl says if they turn what they are eating into eggs we will all be living on them. They really are lovely birds. They walk about as if they are tied together. Fred said he will sink a half-barrel in the corner of their yard for them so they have some water to splash about in, even if it is only a little, otherwise they will be unhappy and we can't have that.

WEDNESDAY 8th

Fred asked if I would like a few extra pigeons this week as someone who had asked him for some was away unexpected. I gave him some eggs in exchange. They will come in handy for the guests at the pub. They are plump birds and will make good pies. Mrs. Wentworth invited me to tea to meet some friends of hers from London, who are staying for a few more days. One of them, a Mrs. Campbell, has a farm in Shropshire and she was telling me about her livestock. She keeps a dairy herd and chickens. Another, Catherine Jones, is an army nurse in her late twenties, a sort of instructor from what she was saying, who is training girls in first aid. I said that they are certainly going to be needed with all these raids we have been getting. I told her how I was in Clapham a few weeks ago. I just mentioned in passing about what the young constable had said about the hot lead dripping off the roof and Miss Jones told me she had heard of a few similar cases. She had been caught in a raid in London when she was on leave and she remarked how her abiding memory, apart from the terrible things that happened to the people, was how quiet it always seemed after a bomb had dropped, as if the city was holding its breath. I asked her if she had any trouble finding girls and she told me that as far as she knew there were more than enough volunteering. There were quite a few she had trained who had tried to get places as land girls and when they could not they volunteered for nurse training. She said how quickly some of the girls grew up during their training. They came as girls and, all of a sudden, they were responsible adults doing one of the most difficult and harrowing jobs in the world and a credit to their country. She also told me that a great many more nurses will be needed soon as people who are in important war jobs, if they are ill, will be offered nursing in their lodgings so as not to have to take them away to hospital. She said she didn't think it was a good idea but the war forces compromise on all of us.

THURSDAY 9th

Mrs. Wentworth came round this evening, just gone seven. She is driving Catherine Jones back to her home in Edmonton on Tuesday and wondered if I would like to go with her as she would like the company on the way back. I said I rather liked the idea of an outing. Doris was saying how she heard we may have the bacon ration cut by three pence. When I told Jack he said that he wished he could get hold of a pig to fatten. I told him that we would be alright as the ducks and chickens would be giving us more than enough for our breakfast and he likes fried bread and mushrooms more than bacon anyway.

FRIDAY 10th

I can't believe it, and neither can anyone else, five ducks and three huge eggs. Fred was dead right, we have eggs by the end of the week. I gave one to him for all his advice. He said that it is not unheard of for a good Runner duck to lay two-hundred eggs in twelve months if they are happy. Jack and I had the other two for our tea with one of the brown loaves I baked this afternoon. They were delicious. What would I do without young Freddie and his generosity? I'll make him a steak and kidney pudding next week if I can get the makings. It is his favourite. Stanley was reading about the prisoners we have taken in Libya, over fifty thousand I think he said. I can't take in that many people. What will they do with them all? Where will they put them and what will they feed them on? We heard a plane going over at about ten o'clock tonight. It was south of here and flying east very low by the sound of it. Stanley said it sounded like a single engine. Jack said he would find out in the morning if Harry, who is standing in for him this week, saw where it went. Things like that make me feel nervous, wondering what it was up to and if it was ours. Talking of the platoon, I hope Mavis managed on her own tonight with the soup.

SATURDAY 11th

Sammy Webster came in for a few things on his way back to 'C' (*Coltishall*). I had some of his favourite buns so he bought some for him and his mates. He told me that Keith, the young lad that was posted here the same time he was, was posted abroad three weeks ago. I had not seen Sammy for over two months, he has been away training. I suppose with so many new things being invented there is a lot of extra things to be learned. Mrs. Wentworth says that we have some of the best brains in this country and they will be very important in helping to win the war.

SUNDAY 12th

Fred gave me some of his special broad bean seeds and said that I should get them in as soon as I can. Mrs. Wentworth said that weather permitting, we will make an early start to Edmonton on Tuesday morning. We should get back sometime in the evening all being well.

MONDAY 13th

One of the men from Jack's sub-section (of the Home Guard) has been called up, the second this month. Dorothy Roger's boy is taking his place. Tuesday is Jack's night off this week so I will ask Mavis to see after his food as I will not be back in time. It looks as if it will be a cold old week this week. Went with George into Dereham today to pick up a few things for Doris and Mrs. Wentworth from Kingston's. Fred was out last night and I have two brace of plump birds that I didn't have this morning. I may make some game soup for the guests at the pub, although they are Londoners and probably would not appreciate it, but I will ask. Stanley loves pheasant since he has been here and there is nothing he likes better for his supper, or packed up when he is out with Jack, than cold pheasant in his sandwiches. The Southampton has been badly damaged, Stanley was wondering about Eddie Mack who was with him on a ship a few years back, he had heard that he was on the Southampton.

'ROSIE THE RIVETTER'
THE FEMALE STRENGTH
BEHIND THE INDUSTRIAL
WORK FORCE

WEDNESDAY 14th

I did not get back from Edmonton until eleven o'clock last night. I enjoyed the day out even though the weather was bad. Catherine was full of stories about her nursing life which I will try to remember and write down when I have the time. She is involved in the King Edward Hospital Fund for London as well as with the Red Cross and St. John's. She was telling me about all the good work they are able to do now for the pilots who are badly burned, and about a Dr. Mackindoe. She said that not that long ago some of the people with terrible burns, like he is treating, would have died. Catherine says that what he is doing is almost a miracle. She is trying to encourage as many girls as she can to take up nursing. Even though some say that girls are needed to do other war work in the factories and on the farms, she has to recruit so many because some are not able to stick with nursing. It is a very difficult job and takes a very courageous nature to face some of the things that they are facing these days. I can only imagine what they have to face after the bombing. We were so late getting back as Catherine insisted we stay for a bite to eat. We had what is always welcome on a cold night, welsh rarebit, and very good it was too. We saw a lot of soldiers about on our way back. I was so tired.

ESSENTIAL JOBS IN THE WARTIME MANUFACTURING INDUSTRIES WERE BEING FILLED BY WOMEN

February 1941

The news from North Africa was the main talking point this month; British forces captured Cyrene and Agordat, and Benghazi was a major victory.

In Norfolk Betty had suspicions that her quacking guests were more intelligent than ducks had any right to be.

SATURDAY 8th

What a busy day. First over to Marjorie's farm to collect some blackout that she does not need. The countryside looked a real picture with the sun shining like it was a spring day. Then back to the pub to put the pies in for the guest's supper. Spent a few minutes with the ducks, I told Beryl I swear they can understand what we are saying. They stood there with their heads on one side and then the other. Four eggs today. That makes a dozen since Monday. And lovely ones they are too. We had one each for tea, Stanley and me. I left one for Jack and Mr. Head on the way home. Stanley and me got back late from the pub tonight. I was serving behind the bar. We were all listening to the news about Benghazi. According to the wireless it is a major victory for the Army of the Nile. Mrs. Wentworth has always said that General Wavell is one of the best generals we have and she has been proved right. Jack said that it was a clever thing to have done, to retreat and fall back on reinforcements and supplies. The Italians did not know what had hit them.

March 1941

Spring arrived in Norfolk and with it the usual optimism. The Lend Lease Bill was signed with the USA. The Italians started their offensive in Albania. Some progress was made by British troops as they regained British Somaliland and Berbera.

Betty contemplated the benefits of duck-keeping and more complex issues.

MARCH 1st

I have had a busy time at Mrs. Wentworth's as she has had a houseful. Most of them were people who work with Mr. Wentworth. All very serious. I cooked them a huge omelette with some of the ducks eggs and dried herbs. It went down very well.

UNDATED

At the meeting tonight Mrs. Wentworth had a friend explain the 'lend lease' business to us. It is all very complicated but as I understand it, it is something like this; Mr. Roosevelt wants to help us but can't because his country does not want to get involved in the war. So he is going to lend us the weapons, ships and things that we need but cannot afford now, and we pay for them after we put Hitler in his place. Good manners stop me from saying where that is exactly. I think most of us understood, Mrs. Wentworth said that Mr. Roosevelt is one of the best friends we have in this time of need.

April 1941

The battles in the Balkans continued. However, everyone knew that the outcome of the war would be decided by matters occurring over, and in, the English Channel. Germany rebuilt her air power on the French side and this month continued to pound London.

In Norfolk, Easter arrived with the promise of better days to come.

THURSDAY 10th

Went for a walk with Sarah Bradley who was here visiting George. She was bombed out last year and is still living in one room in the East End. Bob, her husband, is on leave and has gone to see his brother in Reading to see if he can find somewhere better for her to move into. The landlord she has at the moment is little better than a crook from what she has told me about how he treats his tenants. How they get away with it I just don't know. When I was touring the halls I can't remember any landlady or landlord being what you would call bad. Eccentric, awkward and often mean but usually good-hearted deep down and dependable when they had to be. Baked some fancy cakes for the shop and a huge pile of hot cross buns for the pub, the shop and the rest of us. Mr. Head likes his for breakfast on Good Friday. He tells me that he has had hot cross buns for breakfast every year since he can remember. The only time he missed was when he was in France. All the rooms are full for the weekend. Mavis is doing the cooking and seeing to the guests. She is turning in to a very efficient 'housekeeper' at the pub.

FRIDAY 11th (GOOD FRIDAY)

Took Mr. Head his hot-cross buns. He was looking forward to them. I managed to get him some extra butter for a treat.

SATURDAY 19th

I went to Mrs. Wentworth's today to pick up some books and she told me that someone telephoned her this morning to tell her that Virginia Woolf has been found drowned in a river. She was a friend of Mrs. Wentworth's mother.

SUNDAY 20th

Spent the best part of the day giving the pub rooms a good old going over. They are fully booked for the next three weeks. Stanley was reading about Wednesday night's big raid on London. The fires were very bad but they managed to keep them under control. It sounds as if the fire-watchers and AFS did their usual good job. I often think about what we saw last year.

Switch off that **LIGHT !**

LESS LIGHT — MORE PLANES

May 1941

SATURDAY 10th

Helped behind the bar at the pub as Beryl wanted a change and did the dinners for the guests. Young Freddie said that there was a dog running at Haringay on Monday that he had been told could not lose. It is called Toftwood Manuss. He asked us, Jack, George, Stanley and Mr. Head if we would like a bet, as he would place it for us if we did. He said that he was putting all he could afford on, as the dog was sure to win. George said he would think about it. I don't like gambling but Freddie had such a gleam in his eye that I said I would see him in the morning and Jack, Stanley and Mr. Head said they would have a go as well.

MONDAY 12th

I went to pick my money up from the shop this morning and Doris said that she was having a bet on Toftwood Manuss. Mr. Head had been in to tell her about what Freddie had said in the pub and she had given him her bet to give to Freddie. She said that as it has a local name she could not help herself and anyway Freddie would never have told Mr. Head if he thought there was a chance of him losing his money. Even Mavis is having a bet. I think just about every friend of Freddie's is. Stanley used to help train a greyhound a few years back but hardly ever bets these days.

TUESDAY 13th

Mavis came round early with the paper to show me that the greyhound we bet on had won at 100-8. We found out that we have won twelve times what we put on. I would be ashamed to say how much hard earned money I risked and I will never do it again, but it will be very useful to have a bit extra. Stanley is over the moon because he put more on than I did, twice as much I think, and Mr. Head is beside himself and is talking about going on holiday. I know I have said it before but what would we do without young Freddie, he smoothes the way for so many people. He told me that he had had an accumulator with another dog in another race because it had the same name as his auntie and had won more money than he had ever had before. I told him to put it away for a rainy day and to stop his betting while he was ahead. He said that that was exactly what he was going to do, as he has to work hard for everything he gets. He is paying us our money before opening time at the pub tomorrow evening. What all this is about Rudolph Hess coming here I just can't work out. George says that he had some idea about trying to make peace with us which is just plain daft to me. How can he think we will make peace after the terrible things the Germans have done. As I said to George and the rest of them in the pub, there won't be any peace made with the Germans. We will give them the kind of thrashing that bullies understand even if it takes years. They've bombed our cities and towns, killed innocent people here and heaven only knows what they are doing in other countries, but we can guess as we all hear stories and some of them must be true.

WEDNESDAY 14th

Now that George has joined the Home Guard, Beryl has said that she will be needing to get some help in when she's busy, but as I said it is only once a week or so mostly. I have said that I could use a bit extra and Mavis is willing to help out when she can. I told Beryl that between us we can manage easily and there is no need for her to worry. Even when she has to go and see to her mother we will have no problems at all making sure things are looked after. I can always stay for the night if necessary and Stanley is not unacquainted with the ways of the cellar-man, and with him not being able to join the Home Guard he will be glad to help out. I don't think he will be going back to Clapham for a while yet. It's funny how things are working out. I never would have believed that an old sea dog like Stanley would be happy to think about working in a pub. But when I mentioned it to him he said he would love it. I had an unexpected visit from Tommy Lever as he has a spot of leave due and is off to see his parents. He came round to give me a newspaper cutting about the big raid on Hamburg on Saturday. He told me that Bob Stockwell was on it and got back safe apart from a shrapnel splinter he picked up from some bad flak on the way home. Five duck eggs today. What with the chickens as well we've never had so many. The gentleman staying at the pub asked if he could have a duck egg boiled for his tea tomorrow. He said it would be the first time he had had one since he was a boy growing up near Exeter. Jack has had to get a new part for his van, something is wrong with the steering and it shakes his teeth he says.

THURSDAY 29th

I had a couple of hours baking at Mrs. Wentworth's today. She likes my bread and asked me to show her how to make it as she is trying to be a better cook than she is at the moment. I told her she is very hard on herself and she does well considering that mostly someone has done it for her. As Mrs. Beddowes, who taught me, used to say 'cooking is a practical skill, so the more you do it the better you get'. I got her to do all the bread and told her what to do every step of the way. Although she could not believe it she made bread as good as it comes. I have never seen her look so pleased about anything. I told her that if you can bake good bread it proves that you can bake anything with practise. Before I left she wrote down everything I showed her – I gave her a duck egg for her tea. I never fail to be amazed at some of the people she knows. Her sister, Jane, was at a party a few weeks ago with Brendan Bracken,

Churchill's secretary. I had not realised until then that he was the red haired gentleman I met a few months ago when the house was full. As I said to Mrs. Wentworth today, she need not worry about me, anyone who has spent as long as I have working the halls knows how to be discreet. We would none of us be safe if we told all we saw, and that is more true in wartime than ever. Dunsford used to say that discretion was the oil God gave us to keep the world turning without too many jolts. I was quite frank with her and said that I had guessed that Mr. Wentworth was involved in important war work. She said that she would be most grateful if I would be able to help out sometimes at short notice as sometimes she was caught out and could have half a dozen descend on her with her husband at the drop of a hat. I told her she could rely on me, but sometimes it might be difficult if the pub rooms were full and Mavis was not about. She told me that she had had a big row with her husband about how Churchill became Prime Minister. She said that the Conservative party wanted to have Lord Halifax and not Churchill, and he was just the same as Chamberlain and there would have been no point in changing. She said that it was the Labour party who had insisted on Churchill as the best man for the job and that she would not be supporting the Tories when the war is over. Her husband agrees with her about Churchill but is not very pleased about what she says about the Tories.

Stanley has been following all the news about the Bismarck. He has always said that we should never have allowed these pocket battleships to be built in the first place and should have listened to Churchill. We should have guessed what was going on when they started to buy so much of our scrap iron. That friend of Stanley's, Billy Carberry, who worked in the Pool of London told him that they must be re-arming to want so much. It's a pity the government didn't put two and two together and do something about it. We are being bombed by our own scrap by the sound of it. What my mother used to say was 'a stitch in time saves nine'. This lot is going to cost more than nine stitches in a pair of trousers. Stanley heard that during the invasion of the Low Countries, German paratroopers were wearing Dutch and British uniforms. Shows just what sort of people they are, not even brave enough to wear their own uniforms.

SATURDAY 31st

After sorting out all the jobs that needed doing in his garden Jack spent the afternoon sorting mine out. I just have not had the time lately what with the baking and the rooms to see after. Jennifer Medwin kindly saw after the ducks – ten eggs this week. Doris asked me if I would like to sell some through the shop. I said no because I would rather use them for friends. It is a good way to make sure they get something nourishing inside them what with meat and things being so short. Jack is a hard worker and he seems to be thriving. As does Mr. Head and Fred. I think young Freddie could do with looking at what he eats as he is very thin, like a bone after the dog has finished with it. He says its all the running about that keeps him so spare. He came into the pub today when I was cooking the guest's lunch. I sat him down and made him eat one of my cornish pasties made with all the vegetables that weren't needed. He ate the lot. I shall have to keep an eye on him I think or he will be ill, silly boy. Stanley has started a scrapbook as he has collected some pictures and stories about the Bismarck. I've heard it said that once someone has spent time at sea it's in the blood forever.

June 1941

Some chilling news from the Mediterranean: the embattled island of Crete was in the headlines and people's thoughts...

SUNDAY 1st

The vicar mentioned the battle in Crete and asked us to pray that right would prevail. From what little I have heard though, it is likely that this time it will not. Dougie Webster is in the Mediterranean. Hard to believe that such a good pianist as him should end up with a gun in his hand in a place he will hardly have heard of. Fred brought me some leeks, kale and broccoli which was most welcome. I tried a new recipe with the duck eggs. Beat two eggs with a little milk, a pinch of salt and pepper. Boil the chopped broccoli for five minutes, drain it and put into a pie dish. Pour on the eggs and cook in the oven until just set. This goes well with my straw potatoes. I listened to James Agate on the wireless this afternoon and I'm glad I did. Doris asked me if I would have anything to do with Lord Woolton's idea about jam making. I said it was the daftest idea I have ever heard. I hope the men planning on how to win this war don't talk such nonsense. Mavis asked if I had a picture of Freddie Harrison, the little boy who saved his sister's life during the bombing. I have passed that paper on to Mr. Head. I will ask him to cut it out for her tomorrow. Everyone seems to be starting a scrapbook at the moment, even Mrs. Wentworth.

AN AMERICAN POSTER APPEALING FOR ALL SCRAP METALS

MONDAY 2nd

Young Freddie came round early with some food for the chickens and ducks. I managed to get him to sit still long enough to have a good break-fast – two eggs and cod roes on toast. I will get some weight on him yet. I gave him some of my bread pudding and a pastie for his mid-day meal. The Navy have done another good job getting our boys off Crete. There were terrible things going on there from what it said on the wireless tonight and our boys had paratroopers and dive bombers attacking them. At least they are now safer in Egypt.

TUESDAY 3rd

What a day. Albert woke me up this morning wailing like he was in pain. I could not work out what was wrong with him. I soon found out. I opened the door to let him outside and there was this pig leaning against the door and he rolled backwards into the kitchen. It was a saddle-back and a big one too. He seemed to be quite bewildered. I tried to lead him out with some potatoes but he just sat in the middle of the floor looking about him, sort of lost, poor thing. I went to see Mavis to ask her to fetch Jack for me and Jennifer Medwin was there. She said that she could guess which pig it was. It was one that had been sold by the farm where she works to Eric Tipton. The pig is called Daniel and used to follow Jennifer around the farm. She thought he must have been looking for her. As soon as the pig saw her he followed her into the garden. It was a good thing that I had shut the gate to the vegetable garden as I could have lost the lot. Jennifer walked him back to Eric's place. It is a good home as he doesn't want him for meat, he just likes the company of a pig around his place.

WEDNESDAY 4th

Daniel was back again this morning, sitting in the doorway. I gave him an apple and walked him back to Eric, who was on his way up the road looking for him. He is a lovely old pig. His tail is so curly it almost has a knot in it. I told Eric that he must be more careful as there are people about who would like to get their hands on a pig like him. Eric said that he hadn't finished strengthening his fence into the big field yet but when he has he will not get out so easily. Fred brought me a rabbit and a hare. I shall have the rabbit and jug the hare for the guests. Two commercials in this week until Friday morning and a couple visiting people in Wymondham for the weekend. Went to see Mrs. Wentworth about the meeting tomorrow. She showed me some photographs of her and her husband that were taken on holiday in Crete a few years ago. Some of them were taken on board their ship in the Kithera Straits, where the battle took place. Mrs. Wentworth said that it was strange to think of such a beautiful, warm place as the scene of such terrible sights. She seemed very sad about it all. To take her mind of it I asked her how she got on in Hornsey last week. She said that she was very impressed by Captain Gamman. He was thinking about how we must change things when the war is over. There are not enough people thinking about that, or if they are, they are keeping silent about it, which is not for the good. Mr. Wentworth was not pleased about her canvassing for Captain Gamman, as she made it clear that she was no longer supporting the Conservative party, and she was supporting the man and not his party. Mr. Wentworth was morose all weekend over it. Captain Barnes arrived just as I was leaving, such a polite young man with the most distinguished nose I have ever seen. He would be a proper looking matinee idol if he had been in the theatre. He is getting to be a familiar face, perhaps a bit too familiar for the good of things. Young Freddie brought me a sack of new potatoes for Mavis, Mr. Head and the pub in exchange for a dozen eggs. Jack is standing in for Bert tonight who is away, and I packed him up some tomato sandwiches and a meat, potato and onion pastie which he likes. Freddie had Tyke with him who has grown into a lovely dog with a nice nature. Even Albert gets on well with him, which is unusual for Albert.

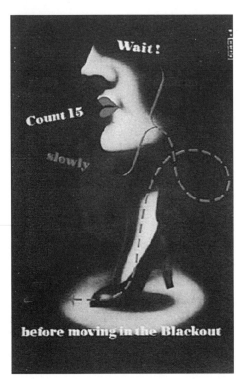

STEP BY STEP IN THE **BLACKOUT**

THURSDAY 5th

Up early to go to Norwich with George. He had to pick up some wood
for shelves that he has to replace in his cellar. I went to see Gladys in
her shop to see if there was any material for some new curtains. Mine
are nearly falling off their rings. I should have replaced them ages ago
but what with one thing and another. All she had was some wine red
cotton, which is alright but a bit dark. Still, it will do the job and may
even help with the blackout. I bumped into Able Armitage in Tombland.
He is staying at his brother's for a few days before going overseas. Bit
of a change from working in the bank I said. He says he enjoys the army
and is thinking of staying in when the war is over as he says that going
back to working in a stuffy old bank does not appeal to him anymore,

and never did when he thinks about it. Did some cleaning and tidying of the rooms at the pub and changed the flowers. I did a salad for the guests as I went to the meeting at Mrs. Wentworth's this evening. We had a talk about the housing situation now and after the war. A friend of hers used to be a billeting officer and she told us about how difficult it was for ordinary people to cope when they were bombed out. Most of them don't have the money to pay removal men and if they did they have nowhere to move to. Even if they managed to find a room or two for themselves there was nowhere for them to put their things, what was left of them. I know for a fact that it is not easy to get a home together at the best of times for ordinary people, and to have to get rid of everything because you have nowhere to put them, and then have to start again is terrible. As Mrs. Wentworth told me as I was leaving, friends of hers who are well off and well connected who have been bombed out just have to ask their friends for some cellar space until they can buy somewhere else to live, or even stay with friends in the country. As she said, money makes all the difference and that is hardly fair considering how the poorer of the country are sacrificing as much, if not more, than anyone else these days. She is writing to someone in the government about the unfairness of it all. We were shown some photographs of some of the places where the bombed out are having to stay. It looks terrible. Imagine having children to look after, to cook and clean for and having no running water. It makes you realise how much worse it is to live in the cities in this war. We all came away with food for thought. I asked for some of the photographs for my scrapbook.

SUNDAY 8th

Mrs. Wentworth gave me a lift to church and asked me back to hers for a cup of tea. She told me she is having some friends to stay this week and she would like me to meet them. Two of them work at the Ealing film studios and she is sure we would have a lot to talk about. I told her a while ago about John Watts who was a friend of mine who is an electrician there. He used to work at the cinema in Oxford Street before he went to Ealing. The last I heard he was hoping to work with Tommy

Trinder, a well mannered young man. I remember having some good laughs with him and my Alfred. Jennifer, Ellen and I went for our walk with Daniel. We took him along the old footpath all the way to Fenn's Barns. He had a lovely time rooting about in the hedges and ditches. When we said 'Come on Daniel' he came as well as any dog would. He trotted along behind us as good as gold. We stopped to eat our sandwiches by the round pond. I wondered if Daniel would jump in for a swim but he just sat down with his face up to the sun. I had taken along some apples for him and he enjoyed them more than anything I think. Ellen told me that this was the first time she had spent any time in the country and had not seen a real live pig until she joined up. I wish I had had a camera with me. It was such a picture with the three of us sitting there with Daniel on the end like a portly gentleman, looking this way and that at whichever of us was talking at the time. I think he understands every word we say. We got back home just as a chilly breeze got up. Went to see to the guests at the pub and walked home with Jack. He is off to market this week and is picking some wood up from Ted for the fencing job at Garvestone. I had a count up tonight and I am surprised at how much I have been able to put away from my cooking, baking and share of the rooms money. I can't remember having so much before. If I go on at this rate I shall be doing well. What would Alfred have said I wonder? Stanley has been following the progress of the search for the Prinze Eugen which has been found at Brest, which is being attacked by us. Stanley said he would have put money on her making a run for the Atlantic.

July 1941

The Anglo-Russian mutual assistance treaty was signed, not something the Nazi high command were at all comfortable with – the words 'Russian Front' became synonymous with terror for them. Later this month Germany bombed Moscow.

TUESDAY 1st

Jennifer has asked me if I would like to go for a walk with her and Ellen Motram, the new land girl at her farm, tomorrow afternoon. They are taking Daniel with them. What a sight we will make going down the lane. I said I would make a few sandwiches and we can take our time, it being so hot.

WEDNESDAY 2nd

Saw Robert 'T' in Wymondham today, I went there with Mrs. Wentworth to do some shopping, he looked very tired and I said he should be getting some rest. I asked him over one evening for supper when he can find the time. I asked if he had seen Sandy 'Mac' (believed to be in Blenheims) from WR (West Raynham). He told me that he had had a spot of bother over in Germany and was on leave for a while. He promised me he was alright but badly shaken up and in better shape than he left his target, which is what Sandy thought was more important. He did not have his address so I can't write. Mrs. Wentworth asked me if I would get the tea for her guests as she had to pick two of them up from Norwich and as there was no one at her house I would be able to look after the others if they arrived early, which two of them did. We had a salad with the egg and bacon pie I made yesterday. I did not stay late as I had promised to make some sandwiches for the platoon as Mabel is having her in-laws to stay for the week. I had a quick word with Peter Cable, the man who works at Ealing, and mentioned a few names but he did not know any of them unfortunately, but like he said he may not know them by name but would by sight or nickname. He knows Tommy Trinder of course. Young Freddie brought some food for the chickens and ducks. I have quite a supply now. Jack said I must check it regularly for rats and mice. The ducks never cease to surprise everyone. We seem to have more and more eggs from them every week. I put it down to Fred being such an expert on how to look after and feed them, and Jennifer's care and attention. She spends hours with them when she wants some peace and quiet to read, sitting in her deck chair on the little lawn beside their house. She has even planted some flowers along the wall to brighten it up. I gave her some of my aster and dahlia plants to put in. I told her we will have the guests fighting to sunbathe out there before long. On a hot day the warm air rolling off the high field feels really pleasant, and the view is nice too, all those lovely old oaks and thorn hedges. I like it when we have a good show of poppies up there, like a couple of years ago.

THURSDAY 3rd

Young Freddie came round for his tea. I saw him in Watton this afternoon and made him promise me he would. Honestly, I have seen more meat on a jockey's whip. He tucked in to one of my meat and onion pasties with some salad. He gave me a lovely military type raincoat for Stanley. He said someone gave it to him as payment for some goods. I listened to the Ministry of Food programme this morning. They talk to us as if we are silly.

SATURDAY 5th

Mrs. Wentworth asked me if I would pick her meat up from the butcher's today. There was a notice behind the counter asking people not to ask for more than their ration. I think it was cut from the paper. I can't understand some people. Don't they understand how much trouble our boys have to go to, to get the meat here in the first place from overseas? Had a nice evening in the garden at the pub. We had a few hands of whist. Young Freddie turned up just after eight o'clock and insisted on paying for more than his share. Whenever Freddie and Mr. Head are in the pub at the same time you can be sure Mr. Head has to be seen home singing. Stanley and I got back here just after half past eleven. Jack had left a message to say that he was going to Garvestone in the morning and not to expect him for his dinner. I think he is going to give an estimate for fixing the Carver's long fence, though I can't be sure.

A GROUP OF **LAND ARMY** GIRLS. AN ESSENTIAL FORCE IN THE WAR EFFORT

SUNDAY 13th

I must not forget to register (for rationing purposes), the last day is the 19th and I have forgotten to remind Mr. Head as he does forget so.

August 1941

The skies were quieter this year than last, and summer in Norfolk was at it's best.

FRIDAY 1st

I took everything slowly today. I never complain about the weather being hot as I have spent so many days and nights trying to keep warm on tour. I had a quiet time at the pub, there was a good crowd in this morning. I made some of my ginger beer for Jennifer and her friends. They took a couple of corked up jugs away with them for the afternoon. There's nothing like ginger beer on a summer's day. Jack was on duty this afternoon and I took him some sandwiches and beer. I don't think that he should drink on duty but I am sure no one would mind if they knew. Mavis is having a lot of trouble getting a few days off to visit her aunt in Stoke. I told her that it might be better if she left it a while things being as they are. Stoke is a long way at the best of times. I spent a month there once when I was with Bert Atkins and the Two Jimmies. A funny pair they were, I was glad when that job finished. George lit a campfire in the pub garden and we cooked some sausages in the evening.

MONDAY 4th

Stan and Barry from Swanton Morley dropped by this afternoon for a bite to eat and a sit down. They were telling me about how hard they are working at the moment keeping the planes in the air. I asked them about last year and showed them some of the letters I have had from the boys who have moved on. I had a good idea of how close things were last year but hearing it from Stan sent a shiver up my back. Still, we showed old Göering what we thought of him and I bet he doesn't try that again. Mr. Wentworth told me that the war will be fought on shores other than ours. Thank God for the Channel.

WEDNESDAY 6th

One of the guests at the pub asked if I would give him some advice about ducks as he was very taken with mine. Jennifer showed him what she has to do on her list that Fred gave her when we first got them. I told him that we had not been short of eggs since they arrived.

THURSDAY 7th

I had a letter today from Glim about how hard it is to get good food in London without queuing. She says that some shopkeepers are holding back some things for their favourite customers, she enclosed a newspaper cutting. It is about a queue for potatoes and tomatoes. I can't see us going short of those with the likes of Fred and Jack being such good gardeners. It makes me realise how good it is here in the country.

SUNDAY 10th

Freddie came for supper this evening. He is looking very well these days and is putting on weight, which is unusual for him. He said he was glad that nobody else was around because he wanted to tell me what he was doing, as there had been a lot of rumours. He told me he has a lot of people keeping chickens for him all over the place and the eggs he gets from them, in return for getting them the chickens in the first place and the feed, he sells to hotels and restaurants in London, as well as vegetables and the like. He says that they are very grateful for them and he is surprised how much they charge for them. I said I wasn't, but I've been around more than he has. I showed him the cutting Glim sent. He said that he would make a lot more if he could get his hands on some wine. A friend of his in London sold him some from a bombed out pub and he managed to sell it for five times what he paid for it to a posh place in the West End. I told him there will always be money in drink if you can get hold of it.

September 1941

Difficult though it was to believe, it had been a year since the Battle of Britain. Time had passed quickly in Norfolk but not because it had been an enjoyable time; it had been a busy and worrying time as the war raged in distant, and not so distant, places and family and friends were still away from home. A stranger arrived in the village who had a profound effect on some of the people he met.

MONDAY 1st

Mavis and I have spent the day sorting out the jam stock. We have certainly done our bit to see we don't go short. Fred has come up trumps with his strawberries. Freddie came round this afternoon and offered to buy some jam from us as he says that he will have no trouble selling it in London. He is doing very well at the moment and is helping to keep all of us supplied with some surprising little luxuries. He said that he will be bringing a friend of his to see me next week called French George. He is going in to a sort of business partnership. I hope he knows what he is doing.

TUESDAY 2nd

Went into King's Lynn this morning to give Jack a hand with some chickens he was selling. We didn't stop and were back by noon. Helped behind the bar as there was a full-house with the boys from Coltishall. Young Bill 'T' was there which was a surprise. I had heard he had been posted abroad, but he wasn't as he volunteered for special munitions training. Jennifer Medwin came for a walk with me this evening. She had Daniel with her and I gave him some little potatoes I had saved for him. He has a lovely nature and Albert has become quite fond of him. George says she can take him to the pub on Saturday for the party if she wants to. I don't think he would like all the noise though. I am spending tomorrow in my garden as it needs a good tidy up. Mavis is having a day off from work and is seeing to the rooms at the pub.

WEDNESDAY 3rd

Well, I don't know what to think. Freddie saw me in the pub tonight and asked if I could go to his place for a quiet word. Beryl was there and things were quiet so I went with him. French George was at Freddie's and we had a drink together. He is a big man with short blonde hair and talks very briskly. Not unlike the way Henry Smedley who ran the old Empire used to talk. He seems a nice enough chap. He comes from a fishing family near Winterton and has spent a lot of time in France since he was a lad and speaks the language, I do a bit so we had a bit of a laugh. He told me that he misses his friends across the channel and some of them are like his family. He is coming to the party on Saturday.

THURSDAY 4th

Fred gave me a hand with the last of the potatoes. I have done quite well this year, and have some good big ones for baking. The ducks have not been laying quite as well lately but are doing much better now.

FRIDAY 5th

I was up early to get started on the baking for the shop. I should have started it last night but had to help Jennifer out with a little problem she had with her boots. Jack has an early start tomorrow as he has to take a load of goods up to Cromer for young Freddie.

SATURDAY 6th

Had a good day getting things ready for the party tonight which was a good night for everyone. There will be some sore heads in the morning including Mr. Head's. He was on the rum last night that French George brought. I had a nip myself and so did Stanley, he said it tasted like real Navy rum. There is something funny about French George but I can't put my finger on what it is. He reminds me of a character actor I knew in Wolverhampton.

FRIDAY 12th

Had a very busy day at the shop this morning as Doris was away all day. Mavis filled in this afternoon as I had to go to Mrs. Wentworth's to get things ready for the weekend. Mr. Wentworth has one of his secret meetings with some of the top brass. So there was a lot to do, what with cooking for all the drivers and aides who will be coming.

UNDATED

Stanley wants to go home (London) just to see everything is all right there, but I told him to think about it. After all, Newcastle (*the city was bombed on September 30th*) proves that Jerry are still going to have a go at our cities. He's all right here and I don't know why he doesn't move here for good. Cities will not be fit for people to live in for years even after the war is over. Mrs. Wentworth says that we should start thinking about rebuilding our shattered cities now, otherwise doing things in a rush will lead to mistakes.

October 1941

In the big wide world the war ground on; events in the east reached a critical phase; and one of the pivotal points about which the outcome of the conflict was to turn, as the German advance on Moscow led to Stalin declaring a state of siege.

In Norfolk Betty prepared for winter.

SATURDAY 4th

There was a sharp nip in the air this morning. I was up early to sort out some warm clothes for Edna's two boys. Summer has gone, Albert only goes to sleep on his barrel for an hour or two these days, and autumn is here again. The third of the war, I wonder if this will be the last of it. Well, as Jack says, it will end when it ends and there's no point in worrying over it. I don't mind autumn really, there is something to say for every season. Mavis has come on a long way since she has been helping me with the rooms at the pub. George says she will make a cracking good landlady one day, and he's right. She is a good cook now as well. She cooked a steak and kidney pie for Mr. Head last week and it was one of the best I have ever tasted, if not the best. Jack has asked me to go to Dereham market on Friday. Doris won't need me so it will be a day out and I can pop in and see Margaret, I keep promising her I will.

WEDNESDAY 8th

Young Freddie came for his tea tonight and told me some things that I wish he hadn't, and he told me not to tell anyone else. He has no close relatives he can rely on so he told me what he is planning to do with French George. I could hardly believe my ears and I thought he was pulling my leg, but he wasn't.

THURSDAY 9th

Fred has brought some pigeons for the weekend. Billy and Martin from Coltishall came for supper tonight. Their friend Alec was shot up over France and is all right but not very well still. I have sent him some apples by Billy as he is visiting him next week.

THURSDAY 23rd

I am a bit behind with preparing and storing the fruit and vegetables for winter. Beryl has cleaned and scrubbed out the cellar cupboards for the apples and pears. What a fine crop this year. Fred's trees have been weighed down with fruit and as he didn't let many fall of their own and the wind's accord they are all unmarked so will store well. Jack says that it is enough to make sure the apples are not touching each other, and that it is the best and quickest way to lay them up. I will have none of that. I always wrap each one in paper because, as long as I make sure the apples are really perfect when I put them away, I will have no trouble with any of them. My Irish mother was a great one for knowing the best ways to stop food going off. As she used to say her family were nearly wiped out during the potato famine and have learned the best of ways to save food. A talent that will prove very valuable as this war goes on. Freddie thinks that there will be serious food shortages in London this winter. Jennifer Medwin had supper at the pub tonight. She was telling me about how the war seemed to creep up on her in Manchester. The first time she realised we were in for a bad time was when her dad, who is a councilor, came home months before war was declared and told her that they had been talking about where to build air raid shelters and, not long after that, people in her road started to plant vegetables instead of flowers in their front gardens.

FRIDAY 24th

Mrs. Wentworth asked me to help her with her apple and vegetable store today. Her orchards are the best around here. She is using part of the stables for storage this year as two of her horses have been moved to Wales. They were proving to be too much to look after properly now that Bob Thoroughgood has been called up. I don't think he will be coming back after the war as he was always looking for an excuse to get away but could never make up his mind. Looks like Hitler made it up for him. Had a long letter and some handkerchiefs from Glim. She has an interview for a job at the BBC next week. She said that if she got it it would be very convenient as she has been given the use of a flat in Portland Place which is just around the corner from where she would be working. She has had a busy summer doing some filling in at several theatres doing odd jobs and has a pile of autographs for me which she says she will send me for Christmas. Young Freddie came early this morning to tell me he would be going over there with French George in the next two days and would be back in about a week or two, as he would be going to London after he got back. I hope he knows what he is doing.

December 1941

Whenever I see film footage or photographs of houses bombed-out in the war, with the staircases standing resolutely as if defying Hitler in the only way they know how, and jagged walls with the paper of years peeling from them, I always think of the Christmases seen by them – apparently I am not alone in that, from what others have told me.

In Norfolk Betty, her friends and her half-brother Stanley are making preparations for the third festive season of the war.

FRIDAY 5th

Glim has arrived. She apologised for being two weeks early but said she's had enough of London for this year and just packed and left. I can't say I blame her. She is staying at the pub for the time being and will move to the Wentworth's house when I do three days before Christmas.

DECEMBER 7TH 1941
'A DAY THAT WILL LIVE IN INFAMY' WINSTON CHURCHILL

On December 7th, 1941, Japan attacked the American Fleet at Pearl Harbor – in the words of Winston Churchill "A day that will live in infamy".

MONDAY 8th

What news! Mrs. Wentworth said that terrible though it is at least this will do what nobody has been able to do and brought America into the war. She said that Churchill had told Mr. Wentworth a few weeks ago that if America found the will, and a reason, to enter the war Nazism would be crushed in Germany for generations. So now we are not alone.

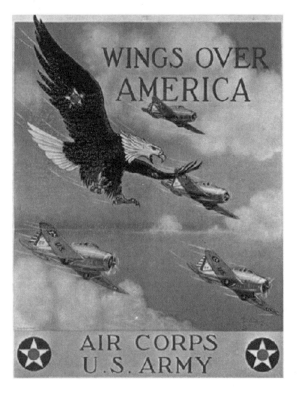

FLYING THE FLAG. A US
RECRUITMENT POSTER

MONDAY 15th

There were some glum faces at the pub today about the Budget. George said that paying for beer and whisky is not as hard as getting hold of the stuff. I thought, though I didn't say anything, Young Freddie never seems to have any trouble and George has the odd bottle to help him out.

THURSDAY 18th

A friend of Glim's arrived today. She telephoned yesterday to say that she had finished work in Portland Place, at the BBC, early and Glim said that as she had nowhere to go for Christmas she could stay with us. The more the merrier as we have a big house to fill.

SATURDAY 20th

The Wentworth's have had to go away early so Mrs. Wentworth dropped the keys to her house off at the pub and asked if I would mind moving in early. Glim has taken Patricia. They will start getting things ready.

TUESDAY 23rd

So, this year for Christmas dinner there will be me, Stanley, Mr. Head, Mavis and her aunt Kate, Beryl, George, Fred, Jack, Young Freddie, French George and about six of the boys from Coltishall and Swanton Morley said they hope they will be able to come. Fred has done his usual best and there will be no shortage of food. We have more pheasants hanging in the outhouse than we can ever eat and Jack has the most enormous turkey I have ever seen and even Fred said that it "don't look natural with legs that size on it". Glim and Patricia have decorated the drawing and dining rooms to look very Christmassy with holly and ivy from the wood and the Victorian decorations that Mrs. Wentworth has inherited from her family. Fred has put a great big Yule log in the middle of the hall and decorated it with tinsel and candles that he made himself. It was nice of the Wentworth's to leave such a lovely big tree to decorate. It goes right to the ceiling.

CHRISTMAS EVE

We had a very quiet night in, just Jack, Glim, Patricia and Jennifer Medwin. We have had to work quite hard to get all the baking done and preparing all the birds was a very long job, it was a good thing that Fred was around to help. Mrs. Wentworth telephoned at five o'clock to wish everyone a happy Christmas and to tell me that she had left a little something in the big cellar for us all and we were to open it tonight. Young Freddie and French George struggled to bring it up because it was a big box. In it was a case of wine with half a dozen bottles of whisky, brandy and rum 'to help things get good and rosy, as Christmas should be even if there is a war on' she said on the Christmas card that she had left with it. And some presents for the boys who we hope will be here tomorrow. Six hip flasks filled with malt whisky. They will go down well.

A Merry Yuletide
May your Christmas be bright and pleasant
Is the wish that I fondly invoke.
I'd like to send you a Christmas present,
But to tell you the truth, I'm broke.

HAPPY CHRISTMAS 1941

CHRISTMAS DAY

It is ten past two in the morning and it has been a lovely day. We sat down for dinner at two o'clock sharp and there were eighteen of us round Mrs. Wentworth's huge table. Glim sang some songs after we had the Christmas pudding and port and Stanley banged out some of the old songs on the piano. After that everyone helped to clear up as quickly as possible. Then we all went for a walk in the woods to blow the cobwebs away. We came back just as it was getting dark and settled down for the evening playing cards, having a few drinks and talking. The boys had to go at about seven o'clock, each as pleased as punch with their presents. They are only lads after all.

I am looking forward to the New Year as I feel sure we have turned the corner and that we won't have another three Christmases under the shadow of war.

January 1942

NEW YEAR'S DAY

Mrs. Wentworth telephoned again this morning. She does not think she will be able to get back for at least three more days. I said I would stay on here until she gets home. Glim will not be going back to London for another week so I won't be on my own. We all saw the New Year in with style last night after a day at the pub seeing to some of the boys. Spirits were very high and more optimistic now that the Americans are going to get stuck in. Glim is going for an audition at Denham film studios. She just missed a small part in 'Hatter's Castle' last year with Deborah Kerr.

TUESDAY 6th

Back home and sorted out. Jack gave Glim and her friend a lift to the station and I went along to wave them off. I invited her to stay during the summer if she is at a loose end. I must say I am looking forward to the warmer days again. January is not my favourite time of year what with February just around the corner.

FRIDAY 16th

Jack and Fred were working in the barn today on the gates and as I was helping Mrs. Wentworth I made them some of my welsh rarebit to warm them up. That has been one of my most popular recipes since I was a girl, and one of the first things I learned to make. It is funny how much better it tastes in very cold weather.

The Japanese seem to be in the papers as much as the Germans these days. They have attacked Kuala Lumpur and Stanley says that this is only the beginning for them.

WEDNESDAY 21st

Young Freddie is back from his little trip. He is a lad. He tells me that it was quite an easy trip across and he did not see any other vessels. He says that French George is a very good sailor as he has been able to sail since he was a boy. He brought me back some lace that was made by one of French George's friends. She makes bonnets for the women in the village where they were staying. Freddie is off to King's Lynn tomorrow to buy some timber for Jack, he is making some new barn doors for Marjorie's husband. A cold old job. I gave him one of the hip flasks that Mrs. Wentworth gave me at Christmas for the Home Guard.

THURSDAY 22nd

Had a letter from Glim to say she arrived home safely and has a new neighbour. She was a neighbour of the AFS woman who was murdered in Gloucester Crescent, Regents Park last October. There were four murders in as many days, I seem to remember. Glim says that her new neighbour has not had a good night's sleep since the murder and couldn't wait to get away from the place.

SATURDAY 31st

Jennifer Medwin came to the pub this evening to help me with the cooking. She has three new girls moving into the district in the next week or so. Fred came in for his usual night time tipple just as Jack and three of his platoon came in for theirs. Fred said that we should have one of our 'feasts' to cheer us up, as things seem a bit on the flat side at the moment with the short days and long cold nights. I had a word with George and he said we should sort something out soon. Perhaps have a 'pigeon pie night'. Fred said he would sort out the pigeons if George would provide the liquid refreshment.

February 1942

This was a quiet time, relatively speaking, for Britain. Enemy raids were practically non-existent, while the Royal Air Force busied itself over Europe. In the Far East the British of Singapore were resolute and in Norway the word 'Quisling' entered the vocabulary as a useful word to express loathing of those who betray.

In Norfolk it looked as if Betty might be on the move again.

SUNDAY 1st

Had a letter from Glim thanking me for Christmas and asking me if I would like to stay with her for a few days in Portland Place for a change. It looks as if she can stay there for as long as she likes as the owners have bought a place in Cornwall and have told her they have no plans to move back to London. It was so cold today that I put two pullovers on. It was a nice sunny day though, and like Spring but for the cold. Freddie is back from another trip across the water. He asked me to take care of two suitcases for him. I put them in the secret cupboard with my valuables. One of the cases was as heavy as lead. I didn't ask what is in it. He told me he will not be going again for some time as he has a lot of work to catch up on here and in London. He offered me a lift to see Glim if I find the time to go. I will have to think about it. I have quite a bit of work on at the pub and Doris has asked me to do two days a week in the shop as a permanent arrangement. I can't really turn away the money, so I don't think I will be able to find the time, but I will see. There is no hurry.

SUNDAY 15th

Fred has been here all day helping me sort out what I will be doing with the garden this year. He has drawn me a plan and written a list of all the jobs for the whole year. I should have good crops of everything if the weather is kind to us. Fred told me that the ducks should start laying in a month or so, although they were producing late last year, almost into winter, which is unusual and they might not do the same again. He had a look at them this afternoon and they are all in fine fettle.

MONDAY 23rd

Mrs. Wentworth had some people staying who have close family in Singapore. What a worry it must be for them. The news from there is not very good at all.

TUESDAY 24th

The new people from Holly Lodge came into the shop to ask me if I could get a sturdy shed made for them. Fred said he would do the job and gave me a pound for getting him the work. I have always liked the look of Holly Lodge, if it had been a little cheaper when I moved here I would have bought it myself. The apple trees would be a godsend at times like these. There are enough to make a good bit of money from.

THURSDAY 26th

Jennifer came round this evening with a huge parcel of fish pieces for Albert. He ran about the kitchen with his tail up like a kitten. Jennifer is training some new girls who arrived last week. It doesn't seem five minutes since she was a new girl herself.

March 1942

Significant, if somewhat outwardly unspectacular, events in the Far East occurred this month; General Wavell met Chiang Kai-shek, General Macarther was on the move and the onslaught upon Malta was about to begin.

In Norfolk the spring sun began to bring to mind the crack of leather on willow and thoughts turned to the sad state of the cricket pavilion.

SUNDAY 1st

Jack has managed to get some green paint for the cricket pavilion. I have said I will lend a hand as I quite like painting. Ted brought some new wood to replace what had gone rotten. Fred says that not much work has been done on it for twenty years at least, apart from the odd lick of paint. I wrote to Glim and said that I will be coming next month for a week. It will give me a chance to see some old friends and give Stanley's place a good going over. Jack told me that there was a rumour that Bob Mortimer had hidden a bag of sovereigns somewhere in the pavilion before he left for France in 1914. As he never came back I suppose they are still there, if ever they were really left in the first place.

UNDATED

I went for a walk with Beryl this afternoon as the weather was so nice. We walked all the way round the big wood and over the bridge. The stream is well up and full of fish. I think we are in for a good summer by the look of it, and I hope I am right as it seems to have been a long winter. I remember the little stream that was near our house when I was a girl and how we used to collect frogs spawn and sticklebacks. It seems like it was only yesterday.

MONDAY 30th

Off to Glim's tomorrow. Two days earlier than I had planned as I am taking Mr. Wentworth up on his offer of a lift as there will only be him and his driver in the car.

April 1942

This was the month in which hell came for a holiday in Norfolk – using Baedeker as a guide. In the early part of the month Betty's thoughts turned to more pleasant and traditional activities, and a trip to the capital.

WEDNESDAY 1st

Doris has ordered twice as many hot cross buns as for last year. I will have to have two solid days baking to get them all done.

FRIDAY 3rd (GOOD FRIDAY)

Spent the day at the pub as the rooms are fully booked and there was much cooking to do. I went to give Mr. Head his hot cross buns for his breakfast, as usual, and then walked to the pub with him as George had asked him to stay for the day. Doris called in to say that she had sold out of buns by ten in the morning.

SUNDAY 5th (EASTER SUNDAY)

Went to church with Mavis and Mrs. Wentworth. It was a nice bright morning and when the sun came out it was quite warm on the face. Jennifer Medwin is coming to see after Albert when I am away so I said it might be a good idea for her to sleep at mine on the odd night if she wants to.

I was woken up in the night by Albert meowing and scrapping. It is unusual for him to come upstairs in the night so I got up to see things were all right. I looked out of the window and saw someone trying to get into the outhouse. I shouted and threw a bottle at them and hit them on the back of the head. They didn't half scream out. They ran off down the road. I told Jack and he said he would tell Bob the local constable, when he sees him. I gave Albert a whole tin of pilchards as a reward.

FRIDAY 10th

Here I am in London again. Not quite the same as the last time I was here, and nowhere near as noisy. Glim met me at the station and brought me to Portland Place. It is a very posh building with some very well off people living here. Just like in the films. I have spent most of the day looking through the photographs Glim has collected. She has dozens and dozens of them, and one I would dearly like of Noel Coward which he autographed for her when she was visiting a friend at a hotel where he was staying. I have not had to lift a finger as Glim and Emily, who comes in to cook every other day, have done everything, even the washing up. We are going to a hotel tomorrow night, where Glim sings sometimes, for a meal. I am looking forward to that.

BACK IN NORFOLK

MONDAY 20th

Back in my own bed again as I write this, and Albert is curled up at the foot of it. I enjoyed myself in London, a change being as good as a rest, but I could never live in a city again.

May 1942

The shockwaves of the Norwich bombing occupied most peoples waking, and no doubt sleeping, moments. It was a time for people to pull together even more than usual.

FRIDAY 1st

Up early to help George to load scones and things. He told me that Mabel Edge has asked him if she can store some of her furniture and things while she finds another place. Poor woman, hers was one of the places bombed flat just off the Dereham Road. She was in her sister's shelter at the time so that's a mercy. Elaine, a Land Girl, is going to the RSPCA at Drayton to see if they need any help. She has heard that there are a lot of pets who need seeing to and looking after. Leonard Pryke said that he would give her a lift there if she can get the time off, she is expecting she will as Billy, who owns the farm where Elaine works, is a dog lover.

SUNDAY 3rd

Everyone who was helping out yesterday was too busy to go to church today. We still have a lot of sorting out to do if we are to help. Jimmy West has taken loads of things to the pub for me to sort through, he can remember how hard he and his family had it when he was a boy I suppose. I can remember the story he told me about how one Christmas, when he was a child, his family had no meat on the table. His father, being too proud for charity, went out early on Christmas morning with only a stick and managed to kill seven rabbits on their seats. Four of them Jimmy's mother cooked for Christmas dinner and three were given away to some neighbours who needed feeding too.

MONDAY 25th

I was remembering something Beveridge said a few months ago about how the British must be fed like an army. He was right, when you think what people may have to put up with when you see what an old city like Norwich has been brought to by two nights of bombing.

UNDATED

It's so terrible to see what has happened to Norwich, I don't know what to say after seeing such sights. So many people not knowing what to do, and only wanting the simplest of things like a change of clothes and being able to make a cup of tea whenever you want. I think it will take a very long while before some of them are back to normal again. I did not say it but I think if it had been me I would have left the city if I had relatives or anyone I could stay with. Mrs. Wentworth was very upset to hear that St. Mary's church was bombed. We stood outside in the pub garden tonight and listened to the bombers flying out. George served the drinks outside and we all cheered as we thought how we were getting our own back for the city. Freddie left some toys and clothes for Elsie and three bottles of whisky for Billy Marsh as he thought he looked like a man who could do with a drink or two. I did not get to bed until two o'clock this morning.

June 1942

In the Pacific the Battle of Midway was to be fought, in North Africa the Eighth Army were forced back to Mersa Matruh and later General Auchinlech took charge. As the month drew to a close Rommel neared El Alamein.

In Norfolk Jack had a mishap and Betty lent a hand.

TUESDAY 2nd

Jack cut his hand badly today and I told him he should get along to the doctor for a stitch or two. Not him though, so I cleaned it and bandaged it. I hope it is all right. I can hardly believe that it is June already and nearly mid-summer's day again.

SUNDAY 7th

The ducks are laying well again and Doris is selling some for me in the shop. Fred has finished digging them a much bigger pond in time or the hot weather and they really are a sight when they start splashing about. They line up like little soldiers waiting their turn. Had several of the boys from Coltishall in the pub tonight. They seem in very good spirits and were talking about the big raid on Essen a few days ago. I can't even begin to imagine what a thousand bomber raid must be like. It must be terrible to be on the wrong end of one. I don't suppose the raids I saw in Clapham were anything like that but were bad enough. When I think back it is a wonder anything can live with so many bombs coming down. Poor old Norwich looks bad enough and that was small by comparison but no worse for the people though. Still, it does not do to dwell on such things, much better to get on with doing what we can to see that we keep everyone's spirits up and win in the end. The odd set-back, however bad it is, is no reason to start feeling miserable.

WEDNESDAY 17th

Had a letter from Glim today. A friend of hers was hurt when an unexploded bomb went off last week. They think it had been there for six months or more. She said quite a few were killed and no end of houses knocked down.

SATURDAY 20th

It looks like being a good growing year. I have more lettuces than I could ever use so I am selling my surplus.

MONDAY 29th

I was helping at Mrs. Wentworth's today and there was a young officer there staying for a few days on leave. He was telling me about the events in North Africa. He sounds very posh but very bright. He said that Rommel was a man who looks as if he will be difficult to beat but that he isn't, as he is not a soldier who is capable of going as far to win as we are. He said that to knock the Nazis for six you have to be prepared to be more aggressive and determined than they are, and we are, because they started it all and we are damned angry that we have had to stop doing what we want to do and travel to God forsaken parts of the world where no Englishman in his right mind would ever go if he didn't have to. And to cap it all they bomb our houses and kill our families and get shirty if we do the same to them. "Well," he said and I wrote this out in Mrs. Wentworths's kitchen so I did not forget it, "we will do the same to them and we will very probably do much, much worse to them. So much worse that when this is all over the German's, and all those who helped them, will bleat about how horrible we have been to them. And I for one will have no sorrow or sympathy for a single one of them because they are evil men and women who have done evil things to innocent people and who have forced civilised people to do terrible things so that even worse things are not done in the future". I will not forget that young man, he had a look of real hate in his eyes that would frighten me if I was a German or anyone who had ever lifted a finger to help them.

July 1942

In North Africa, in July 1942, things started to fall apart for Field Marshall Rommel – who was, incidentally, feeling the effects of numerous ailments, from liver disease to acute catarrh. General Claude Auchinlech was to be the allies instrument to begin Rommel's ultimate defeat, but was not destined to be in at the kill – that honour was waiting for one of Britain's greatest warrior tacticians, Field Marshall Bernard Law Montgomery.

In Norfolk the sun was shining.

WEDNESDAY 1st

Mrs. Wentworth is having a garden party next month and has asked me to go and to bring some friends. Mavis said she will come and Jennifer is trying to get an hour or two off. She asked if she could take Daniel. That would be a thing.

TUESDAY 21st

Had a very lazy day just pottering in the garden and going for a walk with Jennifer to feed the ducks, who are doing very well and laying as well as ever. Fred has done a lovely job on their new pond and it is being well used in this weather with all the splashing about that they do. Beryl being Beryl I had a bit too much sherry and felt quite flushed as it was quite warm in the van coming back. Jennifer certainly likes her gin. I was quite surprised. I hope she is not getting into bad ways. Some of the other girls with her now are a bit on the loud side and, although they mean well, do get a bit out of hand sometimes, so I hear.

WEDNESDAY 29th

What a nice surprise, I have had a letter from Barney Freed. I thought perhaps he was in North Africa, but he was not.

Dear Betty,

Yes, it is me. I hope this finds you well. I got here yesterday and have only just sorted my kit out at last. Do you remember me telling you about Bert Wormold? Well I nearly fell over him last afternoon as I brought my kit into the hut. He was sitting in front of the stove with his legs across the gangway. Trust him to find a warm spot. Like I told you, you will never find Bert standing, sitting or lying in a draught. The last I heard of him before yesterday he was down south somewhere and blow me here he is up the other end of the country. Still, he is a good lad and likes a game of cards. He saw Lennie, you remember Lennie, he was the bloke who drank that bottle of green stuff that George had behind the bar for years and went green himself. Well, Bert saw Lennie a few weeks ago on a train and he told him his family were bombed out last year. They were all in a shelter so nobody was hurt thank goodness. They have all moved up to his Gran's place in Kelso until things sort themselves out.

There is a nice little pub not far from here and the landlord used to be a boxer. He has a face like a well worn boot, from the days when he was boxing in the booths. He has loads and loads of photographs of some of the champions like Dempsey, Max and the like. It looks like some of us might be here for a long time so me and some of the lads are going to try to get a darts team up.

I often think of my stay in Norfolk and Stanley and his boxing yarns. Say hello to him and Beryl for me won't you?

Well must close now and get my head down or I will be dropping my spanner in the morning, and my Sgt Major is funny about things like that. He has a habit of calling people names when they drop things.

Keep smiling,

Barney (Somewhere in England)

August 1942

This was the month when another major player entered the war and Eisenhower dug in; Montgomery took command of the Eighth Army; the name Guadalcanal earnt its violent place in the lexicon of bloodshed and the allies' raid on Dieppe saw more than 3,000 casualties out of a force of 6,000; a curate's egg of a month.

In Norfolk the summer burnt on. We pick up the diary again in early autumn.

September 1942

In North Africa the New Zealanders got stuck in and helped Rommel on his not very merry way; the RAF made their famous day-time low-level Mosquito attack on Gestapo HQ in Oslo; bombing raids on the south coast of England continued and in Norfolk Betty was still pre-occupied with the aftermath of those in Norwich.

FRIDAY 4th

Mrs. Wentworth asked me to go with her and help a family who were bombed out in Norwich. They have only just managed to find some rooms in the city and need all the help they can get. I took Jack with me and we went to Norwich in Mrs. Wentworth's car. She had sent some things ahead in a removals lorry. The family is called Campbell and Mr. Campbell is overseas and they haven't heard from him for a long time. Not that that is anything out of the ordinary these days. Mavis goes months without hearing from her Andy and now doesn't think anything of it. Jack and the lorry driver humped the furniture up the stairs and into the rooms and Mrs. Wentworth and I helped Molly – Mrs. Campbell – with the unpacking. We were all done and dusted and eating jam and scones for tea by half past five.

October 1942

This month the conscription age was lowered to eighteen. Operation 'Torch' commenced, the purpose of which was the invasion of North Africa. The second Battle of El Alamein got underway with an awesomely terrible one thousand-gun bombardment. El Alamein was to prove a major turning point of the war.

In Norfolk most people's thoughts were with the men fighting in the desert; and preparations for winter were well in hand.

FRIDAY 2nd

I said to Jack this evening how quickly winter is upon us this year. It was quite miserable and cold coming home from the pub tonight. I saw Daphne Wright outside Kingston's this morning and she told me her Frank is in North Africa, and she hardly dare listen to the wireless, things being what they are. Some young Americans spent the evening at the pub. Jack was trying to explain darts to them but they said it was "overly complicated" and gave up trying after a while. One of them, a young dark boy called Garcia, said he was finding the cold weather hard to get used to but that he liked the fresh air. He told me he was brought up in New York after his family had moved there from Virginia when he was two.

FRIDAY 9th

I had the usual yearly letter from Teddy Westerby. It brought to mind 'Roaring' Bob Windsor, there was a lad if ever there was one. He turned up for an audition for an opening spot in a show Larry Fuller was putting on in Rochdale. I was very young then and learning the ropes. Larry was late for the audition so Bob Windsor said that he would nip next door to the pub, as the landlord was an old friend, for a quick one to settle his nerves. He kept popping back to see if Larry had turned up, and this went on for two hours. Larry got there two and a half hours late. Bob came in just as the second turn was being auditioned and went on third. He was as drunk as drunk could be, but soldiered on and just about got through his piece, and told his jokes and sang his song. Larry loved it and gave him the job. Bob had to have a drink or two every time he went on after that because he couldn't sing the song to Larry's liking when he was sober. Poor old Bob. I wonder where he is now.

"These simple things..."

In the quiet of the evening, waiting perhaps for the nine o'clock news. All that is peaceful and restful is centred in the room, around the fireside.

Such simple ordinary things—a thrilling book, a special chair, the favourite, homely nightcap—OXO.

These are the things that make up home.

PREPARED FROM PRIME RICH BEEF

THE SIMPLE THINGS IN LIFE .
SIPPING OXO AND LISTENING
TO THE RADIO

November 1942

In North Africa Montgomery was finally able to say that the German and Italian armies were convincingly smashed. Later this month the Eighth Army reached Benghazi. As the winter in Leningrad started to bite the Russians bit back even harder at the Germans. In Britain all production of private cars was halted.

In Norfolk Betty had to change her plans to do a bit of 'Nightingaling' and writes of nothing else in her diary.

FRIDAY 27th

Fred came round early this morning before I was up. Mr. Head had a nasty turn in the night and Fred sent for the doctor. It is his chest again. These cold damp mornings don't do him any good at all. I went to see him just after nine and he did look very poorly. It is just one of those weeks this week with everyone being very busy or away. George is all alone at the pub as Beryl is away seeing her sister in Rotherham and Mavis is not getting back much before seven every night with so many being away with colds. I have told Doris that I will have to stay with Mr. Head as much as I can so I will not be able to help in the shop.

SATURDAY 28th

Had to call the doctor in again this afternoon. Mr. Head was breathing so badly I thought we were going to lose him. The doctor said that he was not doing as well as he would hope. It is not a very bad cold but with his lungs being so bad anyway he is very worried. It is such a shame. I have made a bed up in the front room and will stay here as long as I have to. Jack is going into Fakenham tomorrow and is going to do the shopping. Doris has said that she can do without the baking this week as things are slow. She is going to make a few trays of scones herself. Young Freddie sent a bottle of brandy round with Georgie Smith who is doing some odd jobs around and about these days to help his family out. He told me Freddie would be away for a week or two but hoped he would be back for Christmas. It is a very cold night as I write this and I have had to make the fire up to keep the house warm. Mr. Head's house is so draughty I can hardly believe he can ever be warm, and can hardly wonder he has a bad chest.

SUNDAY 29th

Mr. Head had a very bad night and the doctor said that we should prepare ourselves for the worst. His breathing is very bad and he is not able to recognise anyone today.

December 1942

The third full year of the war drew to a close. In the various theatres of conflict around the globe thoughts turned to home, Christmases past and the uncertainty of Christmases yet to come. In Britain Beveridge drew up his plans for the Welfare State, in Norfolk Betty and her friends were preoccupied with the welfare of a veteran of the last war.

TUESDAY 1st

A damp night last night and Mr. Head's sleep was very disturbed. Jennifer stayed with him for some of the time while I went for a bite to eat at the pub. The doctor said that all we can do is wait. I had some jobs to do at my house this morning and Beryl was very kind and said she would sit with Mr. Head for a couple of hours. Doris said that when her uncle Barney had a turn like Mr. Head, which is, after all said and done, just a very bad cold made a lot worse by him having been gassed in the last war, her aunt used to make up some concoctions of almond, calomel and ipecacuanha. She wondered if it would help. Seeing as how he has been so bad for so long I said it would likely do no harm. She made some up and brought it round this evening at about six o'clock and I gave Mr. Head a little straight away. He seemed very weak. Doris said to give him just a little every half an hour or so. Sometimes these old remedies are the best and anyway nothing else seems to have worked.

FRIDAY 4th

The doctor was very pleased with Mr. Head this morning. He is sitting up in bed and even had some breakfast, and a good one at that. His breathing is almost back to normal and his colour is coming back a treat. I didn't dare tell the doctor about Doris's mixture as medical types can get funny about things like that. Still, what does it matter as long as the patient gets better?

SATURDAY 5th

If I hadn't seen it with my own eyes I would not have believed it. Mr. Head was up and about and even wanted to go for a walk. But I said that he should not over do things until he is back to full health and it is a bit on the cold and damp side out. He had a fair old drop of some of the whiskey young Freddie brought round for him. I can start thinking about Christmas now as I haven't done anything yet. All I know is that I shall be spending it at the pub this year.

HAPPY CHRISTMAS 1942

CHRISTMAS EVE

Jack has the turkey and Fred has done his stuff again this year and provided three brace of pheasants to make sure we have enough to go round. We are having turkey and pheasant, sprouts, roast potatoes, artichokes, peas, carrots, bread sauce of course, followed by Christmas pudding and my Christmas pie. We have put two of the big tables together in the back room and, like the year before last, we will have Christmas dinner at two o'clock but will keep something ready for any of the boys who said they would like to come but don't know exactly what they will be doing.

Jennifer and Mavis and one of the new Land Girls, Annie, spent yesterday decorating the pub and the back room and it looks very seasonal. Jennifer has a Victorian Christmas card and she has used that as a guide. Fred's tree fills the corner of the room and when the fire is lit in the grate it all looks very homely. What we all need at Christmas and especially those who are away from their loved ones.

DAY AFTER BOXING DAY

The busiest Christmas of the war. We had people coming in from the middle of the morning. There were fifteen of us for Christmas dinner and it was a fine spread by any standards. Mrs. Wentworth sent six bottles of wine and by the middle of the afternoon some of the boys were drifting in for a bite to eat and a drop of cheer. Later on Beryl knocked out some songs on the piano and by eleven o'clock everyone was having a rare old time. Including Mr. Head who has perked up no end, Freddie's whiskey again I think. Old soldiers like him are tough, like our young ones thank goodness.

A very happy Christmas we had to be sure, and here is to a very happy and perhaps peaceful 1943.

January 1943

Although the American presence had been building throughout 1942, it was not until this year that the realisation of the influence this 'benevolent invasion' would have sank in – not only on the ultimate outcome of the war but also on the people with whom they would come into contact. East Anglia was to be home to more Americans than any other area of the country. Even today the signs of the American presence can be seen in the many disused WWII USAAF airbases spread throughout the area – Shipdham, Wendling and Hethel to name just three.

In the wider world events were moving inexorably in the allies favour in Libya, Russia, New Guinea and Guadalcanal.

On a banner behind the bar at George's pub, for the New Year gathering, were written – more in hope than belief – 'Peace in 1943'.

The start of the New Year bought a request to make some American 'fly boys' feel welcome.

FRIDAY 8th

Jack came round with Brian and Sid after Home Guard tonight and Sid's feet were soaked through and he said he could hardly feel them they were so cold. He had been standing in a puddle up to his ankles down by Coopers and his boots were not up to it. Jack told him that he should take more time with the dubbin.

SATURDAY 9th

Mrs. Wentworth came to the shop today to ask if I would be able to cook for some people she has coming next weekend to have a meeting with Mr. Wentworth. They are American Air Force officers and she wants me to cook something different for them, something special and British.

February 1943

This month saw the first action of Orde Wingate's 'Chindits' against the Japanese. Winston Churchill said that in his whole life he had only twice been in the same room as men whom he felt to be worthy of the description 'great'; one was T. E. Lawrence (of Arabia), the other Orde Wingate. We should be aware of the special quality of those on the home front who, day in and day out, went about their lives under the most terrible of threats knowing that the most odious of barbarians had a foot in the door to these islands. Those entrusted with the prosecution and ultimate destruction of that barbarian and his minions, also had similar special qualities of determination, single-mindedness and, when necessary, as it often was, brutality that drove fear deep into the enemy. The list of these men is long and includes: Air Chief Marshall 'Bomber' Harris, General Alexander, Field Marshall Montgomery and Air Chief Marshall Dowding, to name but a few. Because of the character of men such as these, those on the home front began to see an end to the hardships and the cold uncertainty of war.

In Norfolk some warriors of a different, and less war-like, nature were on a brief visit.

WEDNESDAY 3rd

There are some young nurses staying at Mrs. Wentworth's for a bit of a holiday. They are very well behaved and smart young women and some of them are not yet twenty. I have said I will help out with the cooking. I am being paid five shillings but it is no inconvenience as it is a joy talking to such bright young things. They remind me of some of the young-sters who I have worked with on the halls. Just like them they are full of faith in the future even though these times are so hard to live in. Fred was out with his gun yesterday and brought me some pheasant, pigeons and rabbits for the pub. George said I could have some for the nurses and suggested I bake them a game pie. By the look of some of those girls they could use building up.

ROYAL NAVY RECRUITMENT POSTER

TUESDAY 9th

I stayed for the evening at Mrs. Wentworth's and the nurses tucked in to the pies. They are a very talkative lot. Mrs. Wentworth says that that is because they have very strict rules where they work. From what they tell me they work very long hours. The young Irish girl, Jean, said that she works ten hours a day for six days a week with half an hour break for a meal. No wonder they look so washed out. I remember that the young lady from the King's Fund, who was here a few months ago, said that one of the things she thought that caused the most hardship to nurses was the uniform and from what I saw of the ones these nurses wear it's not hard to see why. It has a starched collar that is so high it must be terribly uncomfortable, hard and stiff starched cuffs and a silly cap to anyone with any sense, and different in every hospital which means that overworked nurses have to waste time fiddling to get it to look right before they can go on the wards.

TUESDAY 16th

I was talking to a young American airman who came into the pub tonight about the nurses uniforms in this country and asked him if they were the same in America. He told me that American nurses wear overalls. That's a much better idea.

WEDNESDAY 17th

The American airman I was talking to last night came in the pub again tonight and said that he had told some of his mates about the nurses staying with Mrs. Wentworth and they wondered if they would like to go out with them. I said I did not think that would be a very good idea. I think I may have offended him.

March 1943

In North Africa the allies pursued Rommel and took El Hama and Gabes after a bitter battle. Berlin was on the receiving end of massive bombing raids. Churchill, only recently recovered from a chest infection, was pleased to announce a victory in the desert. In Europe the RAF were bombing and attacking anything of the enemy's that moved on rail or road.

CHURCHILL GIVING THE FAMOUS VICTORY SIGN

April 1943

The Eighth Army together with Patton's 2nd Corp. made important progress in North Africa. A major push upon Tunisia began. In Poland the massacre by the Germans of 60,000 Jews in the Warsaw ghetto commenced – one of the foulest crimes in the history of mankind. The Americans were successful in killing the infamous Admiral Yamamoto. Life in Norfolk was uneventful.

May 1943

By any standards this was a memorable month: by the end of it The Afrika Korp was no more; the enemy surrendered in Tunisia; as the threat of invasion receded signposts were permitted once again in the countryside. On May 16th one Wing Commander, Guy Gibson, led the bombers of 617 Squadron on one of the greatest operations of the war – the Dambusting raid on the dams of the Ruhr. At great cost to themselves the Dambusters delivered a blow that proved to be one of the best morale boosters of the war. To give some idea as to the character of Guy Gibson and his men there is a true story of a time when Gibson had flown many missions without a break. He was 'persuaded' to take some leave. However, Gibson, being Gibson, found a squadron who permitted him to 'help out' with training the night fighter force so vital during the blitz. At one stage Winston Churchill was brought in to encourage him to take the rest he so badly needed and whisked him across the Atlantic to tour US bases and talk to the American airmen. On his return, during another enforced 'rest', and according to Sir Arthur 'Bomber' Harris, he was "found in his office with tears in his eyes"; being separated from his men and the battle was "breaking his heart". Sir Arthur later said this: "If there is a Valhalla, Guy Gibson and his band of brothers will be found there at all the parties, seated far above the salt." Who could argue with that?

AMERICAN ANTI NAZI
PROPAGANDA POSTER

MAY 8th

This is my favourite time of the year. Steve Kubrik said that his home in Virginia is like here in the spring. I suppose it must be difficult for these boys not being at home on lovely days like today, and having to go to war every day and not knowing if you or your friends will ever come back. When I think of how many of these brave boys have touched the ground here for the last time it makes my blood run cold. I would like to get my hands on Hitler I really would.

June 1943

News of the legendary 'Dambusters' was welcomed. Much has been said in recent years about this raid on the great dams of the Ruhr. Some have voiced the opinion that they were strategically a waste of time and lives. However, that is with the benefit of hindsight, at the time it was a marvellous piece of news, psychologically it was arguably one of the most important raids of the war.

UNDATED

What news about the dams raid. As Jack said that kind of attack will shorten the war with no doubt at all. Mrs. Wentworth was reading in the paper that the electric power the Germans will lose will slow them down. What with that and all the other good news and because of all the brave young men, I think we can see an end to all this now.

It was a lovely sunset tonight and Jennifer and I sat in the pub garden and had a drink or two. One of the girls she works with gave her a bottle of Gordon's someone had given her and she doesn't drink. Ted had been to the Standard in Dereham this evening and he came and sat with us. He told us that he had had a bit of a fright. He was riding his bike past Moorgate House (Dereham) and heard the ghost ringing the bell. Jennifer said that there are no such things as ghosts but I said I was not so sure. I have seen some very funny things in the places I have worked. Many is the time when I have been clearing up after a show and I have seen and heard things that look like ghosts. Theatricals are superstitious by nature and are the sort that would haunt if anyone can. I have never been frightened by anything like that though. One very funny thing that happened was at the Shepherds Bush Empire. I was in the dressing room talking to myself about how funny Max Miller had been and this voice behind me said that he and Dan Leno were the best there had ever been and I said that I thought Max was the best by far. I turned round and there was nobody there and the door was in front of me. Where that voice came from I just don't know.

July 1943

Following the massive onslaught by the men of Bomber Command the Ruhr was still shaking; Cologne was reported as being in turmoil. July was also memorable for operation 'Gomorrah', a truly horrifying raid on Hamburg; on July 24th 746 aircraft of Bomber Command dropped 2,300 tons of ordnance in less than fifty minutes – this was equivalent to the total tonnage that fell during the five heaviest raids on London. A masterpiece of military planning. The flaming cauldron of destruction that was Hamburg could be seen for two hundred miles. The USAAF followed up the British raid the following day during daylight. On the 28th the British sent yet another mass raid, this time 722 planes, and devastated a reported nine square miles of the city. With hindsight some have said that the raids on Cologne, Dresden and Hamburg should be thought of as war crimes; however, it should be remembered just how badly the picture appeared three years earlier, in 1940. These islands were a whisker away from invasion and had not every advantage been pressed home it is not beyond possibility that Germany could have had the victory Hitler so longed for – and so nearly had. It was obvious in those early and dark days of war that Germany must be defeated at any cost. And as Betty said in her diary "They started it so it is no good them whining". Shortly after one of the worst bombing raids on London, Air Chief Marshal 'Bomber' Harris is famously quoted as having said, while surveying the destruction from the Air Ministry roof, "They have sown the wind, now let them reap the whirlwind". He was as good as his word. The firestorms of Hamburg are still considered one of the most awesome demonstrations of the effectiveness of area bombing and of total war; the effect on German morale was devastating; on the British home front it was quite the reverse.

THE CREW OF THE LEGENDARY **MEMPHIS BELLE**

THURSDAY 1st

I went for a walk with Stanley. Apart from the boys flying over it was lovely and peaceful. Who would have thought that we would ever get used to hundreds and hundreds of bombers flying over day and night?

SATURDAY 10th

We had a good night at the pub. One of the young lads from Shipdham, Hank, was telling me about his 'folks back home' in Texas, and about how the reason he is so big is that he was raised on beef. His dad is a cattle farmer there. I told him that I like a good roast on a Sunday with horseradish sauce. He had never heard of it so I promised to give him some of mine to try.

August 1943

During this month Bomber Command maintained their offensive on German cities; on August 2nd a ninth attack, in eight days, was inflicted upon Hamburg; the Italian evacuation of Sicily began; Rome was declared an open city; a place at the time almost unheard of – Peenemunde – received a visit by almost 600 RAF bombers, the object was to prevent production of the German 'V' weapons; the 23rd saw the largest raid to date on Berlin. This month also saw the first of the infamous raids on the German ball-bearing factories at Schweinfurt – a target that, because of its importance to the Axis war machine, could not be ignored. This led to heavy losses of American bomber crews, of 51 B-17s and B-24s, and caused some serious consideration of daylight bombing.

On August 19th Brendan Bracken, Minister of Information, summed up, in one of the most telling phrases of the war, just what would be necessary to completely defeat the Nazis when he said "Plans are now being made to bomb and burn and ruthlessly destroy in every way available to us the people responsible for this war". Not only were the gloves off, the claws were out.

In Norfolk the summer was being enjoyed and made the most of.

SUNDAY 1st

August always reminds me of the summer season in Blackpool. Hot days walking along the front in good company and the smell of fish and chips making our mouths water. Such happy days for all of us.

MONDAY 23rd

There were a lot of bombers going out today. Stanley reckons they are going to have another go at Hamburg or Berlin. Hearing all that going over reminded me of the Blitz all over again. I wouldn't wish that on anyone but the Germans started it and they have to expect the worst until this is all over, which I hope will be soon.

THURSDAY 26th

I went with Mrs. Wentworth to Norwich today to see Ellen Pryke who used to work with Mavis and has been very poorly since she was bombed out. She is looking better but still has trouble with her nerves, which is hardly surprising when your roof is blown off with you in bed. Mrs. Wentworth had a copy of the Daily Mail from last week and the front page says that we are telling the Germans that they can 'quit or burn'. It looks like we will be bombing them even more than we are already. Mrs. Wentworth thinks that that kind of talk can be as good a weapon as any in war, and after what we and the Americans have been doing to Germany lately they had better believe what we say.

September 1943

In the wider world the war ground on. The RAF again attacked the launching sites of the first of Hitler's 'vengeance' weapons, the V1. The information from the members of the resistance, in occupied territory, was invaluable in assessing just how vital it was to do all that was possible to minimise the threat they posed.

In Norfolk there was still much sadness about the heavy American losses of the Schweinfurt raids.

Betty heard from an old friend who was thinking of visiting with two of his 'associates'.

TUESDAY 7th

I had a letter from dear old Harry Wainwright today. He said that he retired when he saw the war coming and is glad that he did. He lives just outside Ilminster, Somerset, in a cottage he had been saving for. Harry had one of the best dog acts in the business. He was a joy to watch. He asked me to write back to him and tell him where he can stay around here because he wants to come for a short holiday and visit some old friends. I will tell him that he can stay at the pub. George will not mind him bringing his dogs one bit.

MONDAY 20th

There are still very long faces because of all the losses these last weeks. I don't know what to say to them I really don't. Such brave young men who give everything. And those left behind have huge great gaps in their lives with their friends gone. Mrs. Wentworth says, and I think she is right, that the danger they find themselves in makes them numb to such losses and is probably what keeps them from going mad. They are so very young. One of the boys in tonight has just turned 23 and his mates were calling him grandad.

TUESDAY 21st

Harry arrived today with his two little dogs, Polly and Starter. What a sight. In the pub tonight Harry came down for his supper with his dogs hot on his heels and doing everything he did. Harry stands at the bar; Polly and Starter stand at the bar. Harry sits by the fire; Polly and Starter sit by the fire. Harry didn't have to buy a drink all night. He cheered things up no end with some of his stories and his little dogs. By the time he went up to bed he was quite tiddly. As he climbed the stairs Polly and Starter sat at the bottom looking up at Harry, then they looked at each other, then at Harry and then they trotted up after him.

Harry must have played nearly every hall in the country, and not once have I ever heard a bad word said about him. His dogs, little terriers, were the apples of his eye. He always saw to them before anything else. Not like some animal acts and that's a fact. When he was looking for digs he used to take his dogs with him to see if they liked them before he would make up his mind. That didn't go down very well with some landladies. When he started out he was very poor and homeless. He found his first dog sitting by a river with a rope around his little neck and shivering with the cold. That was how it all started for Harry. He taught that little dog to do some tricks and worked hard to make a decent living. One Christmas, when I had a break for a few days because of a bad back, Harry and me, and his dogs, were at the same digs and he told me how he had started in the business and how he was saving all he could to buy a place in the country for him and his dogs. And a few more dogs if everything went well. One of the things that sticks out in my mind is what he called his 'lifesaver'. In the early days when he was very hard-up he could hardly afford enough to keep him and his dogs fed, and he always made sure that they had plenty of lean meat and best biscuits and this meant that very often there was not much left to fill Harry's plate. On these occasions he used to take two very thick slices of bread and soak them in beer. Then, depending on what form of cooking was available, would toast them for a few minutes to get them hot. While they were heating he would melt some grated cheese with a little mustard, some beer a little flour and some milk. He would cook this until it thickened, pour it over the bread and grill, or stand in front of a fire, until it was brown on the top. Harry told me that this kept him going in some bad times. And he knew some bad times, he has worked Berwick when the wind was in the east and times don't get much harder than that, I can tell you.

October 1943

In anticipation of the inevitable, the allies set the wheels in motion for a UN commission on war crimes. Elsewhere the conflict ground on. Close to home there was an attack on a convoy just off the Norfolk coast – four E-boats were sunk and one British trawler.

Betty's thoughts were directed at marshalling the fruits of the summer.

SATURDAY 9th

Jennifer came round tonight for supper as Beryl said she could manage without me, the rooms being vacant, apart from Harry and his friends, until Tuesday. She brought a bottle of gin and we had a good old chinwag. She asked me about my times on the halls and if I missed the life. I told her I didn't miss the hard work, and it was hard I can tell you. But I suppose if I am honest I do miss the people. I remember the Christmases most and the summer seasons. One year my Alfred found this great big piece of canvas. There were yards and yards of it. Him with all his years of painting scenery flats he just had to do something with it. He painted this Christmas scene with reindeer, snow, trees and a log house with yellow light coming out of the windows and Father Christmas dressed in a suit like Max Miller's with flowers all over it. Wherever we were for Christmas, if we had the room, we would hang that up on Christmas Eve. I still have it rolled up in the attic. I haven't felt like looking at it for years but this Christmas I think I will find somewhere for it. It is a waste of Alfred's work not to let people see it.

SUNDAY 17th

Harry has really settled in and is talking about staying for an extra week. Polly and Starter are having a rare old time playing in the fields at the back of the pub. Mrs. Wentworth is spending Christmas in Scotland this year and asked me if I would look after her house while she is away, same as the year before last. I can ask Glim if she would like to come if she is not doing anything else. I could ask Harry as well.

SATURDAY 23rd

We had some of Fred's friends in the pub tonight. They had us all in fits. They told us a story about when some friends of theirs were doing a little sheep stealing. They had to get this sheep past a Home Guard roadblock, so they put a coat around it and plonked a cap on his head. There they were in this lorry with the sheep between them. When they were stopped they said that they had been to the Cressingham Windmill for the evening and 'Charlie' had had one over the eight. The Private who stopped them said that he didn't look to sharp and he ought to see a doctor, then he waved them on. George said that it sounded like the kind of thing Gordon Housego would do, and would let Himmler himself through to save him the bother of being on duty any longer than he had to be.

November 1943

The promise Brendan Bracken made a few weeks ago was being fulfilled in the very heart of Germany. There was a 400-bomber daylight raid, by the USAAF, on Wilhelmshaven and a formidable RAF night attack on Dusseldorf when 2,000 tons of bombs were dropped in less than 28 minutes. Other raids this month on Berlin and Bremen diminished the enemy's will to continue.

In Norfolk Betty was about to meet Monty.

SUNDAY 21st

I had a telephone call at the pub from Harry. He's only been gone a couple of weeks and he wants the room again until next Monday. He must have enjoyed himself. There was a party at the pub tonight for Eddie's birthday. It was his first away from home and Beryl, and Jennifer, having a soft spot for him, laid on some cakes and things. We had a good time. The most smiles there have been for a few weeks.

Ted took my order for firewood. I am a bit later with seeing to it than last year I think. I can't say I am looking forward to the winter this year. I honestly thought that last year would have been the last of this war but here we are about to have the fifth winter. I know it can't last much longer.

Worth a Fortune.

YET she looks for no reward beyond the knowledge of duty staunchly done in the midst of danger and distress. For all that, she'd love an occasional box of FORTUNE to cheer her at her post because the best of all Chocolates are specially made by Caley to combine sheer enjoyment with that extra nutrition she needs to keep her going. Such a luscious assortment in every box! So rich in food value—yet so low in cost!

CALEY'S *Fortune*

IN BOXES ¼lb. 8d. ½lb. 1/4 FULL POUND 2/8 **CHOCOLATES**

FOR THE SOLDIER OF FORTUNE,
MMMMMMM… CALEY'S!

MONDAY 29th

Harry arrived this morning. I know now why he has come back so quickly. He had a surprise for me although 'surprise' is hardly the word for it. He has given me a nine-week-old Aberdeen terrier. I have often thought about getting a dog but worried about Albert as he is set in his ways. But he seems to like young Monty, that's his name. When Harry brought him in and put him on the floor the first thing he did was to scamper over to Albert and lick his nose. Albert didn't seem to mind one bit. Harry told me that Monty was bred by the woman he got Polly and Starter from and is of very good stock. He is certainly a bright little chap. He took a liking to one of my slippers and tried to drag it under the dresser. He was a sight with his little head in the air trying to lift it off the floor as he went. Harry said that he has all the signs of being very intelligent as he has had him for just over a week and he already knows to sit and come. Harry, being Harry, has brought some of his special mixture to feed him on as he says it is important to feed puppies well so they have strong constitutions and strong teeth and bones. Stanley is as pleased as punch as he has always wanted a dog but what with one thing and another he has never had the chance, apart from the time he had a share in a racing dog, but that's not quite the same. Young Freddie was on one of his flying visits and said that he would see to making sure I had "plenty of good stuff for the little'un", him being so keen on dogs that comes as no surprise. I remember how he rescued Tyke after Dunkirk. That seems like a long time ago. I wondered where I should have him sleep but Harry said Monty had to make his own mind up and Polly and Starter would show him how. Harry picked Monty up looked in his little black eyes and said, "where's your bed Monty?". Then he put him down beside Polly and Starter and off they all trotted. They went all over the kitchen, into the scullery, under the stairs and then Polly and Starter bolted upstairs while Monty sat at the foot of the stairs, him being to small to get up them on his own. Harry and me went up, carrying Monty, and there were his two sitting on my bed. "There you be," said Harry, "that's Monty's sleeping arrangements sorted out. A dog should always be given the choice of his bed."

TUESDAY 30th

Harry has been giving me some tips on looking after Monty. I knew most of it of course, but Harry is very fussy about the way dogs are looked after and he knows what he is talking about. He showed me the best way to pick him up and how to make his dinner of brown bread and gravy to go with his meat. He gives Polly and Starter bone marrow soup to keep them strong and it looks as if it does the trick. He is also a firm believer in giving puppies vegetables, as they are as good for them as for us. Harry goes home tomorrow but is coming back for Christmas.

December 1943

The first Bevin Boys were called up to raise coal stocks; USAAF and RAF raids on the enemy continued; German casualties for the year approached a million.

In Norfolk the festive season had, as usual and on time, arrived.

THURSDAY 2nd

Hard to think it is Christmas again, but it is. I will be looking after the Wentworth's house. Most of the boys who come to the pub are going home or have other plans, so we have decided to have a quieter Christmas this year. As it will be Monty's first that is no bad thing.

A MERRY
CHRISTMAS
1943, FROM
MAX MILLER
THE 'CHEEKY
CHAPPY'

CHRISTMAS EVE

Mrs. Wentworth has had Alfred's Christmas picture hung up in her drawing room. It is the first time I have seen it as it should be for so many years Max Miller as Santa with his reindeer and sleigh filled with presents, and at the bottom 'At Christmas smile and make good cheer, for Christmas comes but once a year'. Jennifer and Mavis decorated the room and put up a huge tree that Mrs. Wentworth asked her gardener to cut. Monty was quite taken aback by it and gave it a good look and a sniff, and now when he goes in that room he sits underneath it as if he is saying 'this is mine'. Harry arrived yesterday with Polly and Starter. Monty and them have spent the afternoon running about pulling the decorations all over the place, the little scamps. They had a rare old time. Harry says Monty has grown in the few weeks since he last saw him. He is built like a little tank.

CHRISTMAS DAY

We had a lovely day; Jack, Stanley, Harry, Mavis, Fred, Mr. Head, Jennifer, Freddie and Glim. Fred provided ALL the meats. We had the finest turkey any of us had ever seen. With pheasant and sausages, sprouts from my garden, crisp roast potatoes, artichokes baked with tomatoes, bread sauce, and redcurrant jelly. All followed by Christmas pudding with brandy butter. Monty and Harry's two had far too much to eat and spent the afternoon, after Monty had given Albert his usual good lick, fast asleep snoring by the fire, which Fred had provided some of his special Christmas logs for. We drank to absent friends, and there are many to think about this year, and we all said that we would never forget their sacrifice. Mrs. Wentworth left a present for everyone; a pair of kid gloves for me, a pullover for Stanley and bottles for everyone else. Mavis made Monty a cushion cover with his name on. We all went for a walk later in the afternoon as it was getting dark. That blew the cobwebs away. We had a few drinks and a singsong when we got back and the evening just flew by. We all think that this could be the last Christmas of the war, at least that is what it sounded like from what Roosevelt said last night on the wireless. He said that they were planning the invasion of Europe. What else can that mean? I hope we are all right about that. As I write this, at one o'clock on Boxing day morning, Albert and Monty are lying at the foot of the bed with their heads on Monty's new cushion. I think they enjoyed themselves. Doris is coming tomorrow to do all the cooking as her present to me.

January 1944

At the start of 1944 it was becoming more and more obvious that this would be the year the allies returned to mainland Europe – and the evidence was stacking up: Montgomery had returned to take command of the British Expeditionary Force; Eisenhower assumed command – as Commander in Chief of the Allied Expeditionary Forces in Britain.

The Air Ministry announced the bombing figures for 1943 – a graphic and brutal demonstration of how the enemy have been punished for the Blitz: 153,000 tons of bombs dropped on Germany and a mere 2,400 tons of German bombs dropped on British soil.

In Norfolk a certain terrier was visibly gaining stature.

THURSDAY 6th

Monty gets heavier by the day. All the food he tucks away I can't say I'm surprised. Everyone says they have never seen such a well behaved puppy. He sits when he's told and is no trouble at all. He doesn't chase cats, which I have heard terriers like him normally do. Harry said he was a 'good 'un'.

WEDNESDAY 26th

Fred brought round a big pile of magazines he picked up at a sale a few weeks ago and asked if I would like them. There are Picture Posts, Illustrated and the Sketch. I used to see that a lot of years ago when I was on the halls. Glim told me she had her picture in there once, although I never saw it.

February 1944

As 1944 entered its second month the allies continued to make plans for the invasion of Europe; the setting-up of headquarters for this most formidable of tasks – Supreme Headquarters Allied Expeditionary Forces (SHAEF) – was overseen by Eisenhower.

The largest raid of the war so far, 1,000 bombers drop 2,500 tons on Berlin for 43 aircraft lost. The USAAF and RAF returned to the now notorious ball-bearing factories of Schweinfurt as part of what was called 'Big Week' – part of which was a 2,000-ton night bombing of Stuttgart. At the end of the week 26 German aircraft factories were bombed, this was estimated to have reduced enemy aircraft production by a fifth. In Anzio the enemy continued to fight back, and hard.

American casualties to date were: 19,500 killed, 45,500 wounded, 26,300 missing and 26,700 captured.

Betty was by now getting used to seeing more and more Americans dropping by the Wentworth's, as elsewhere the massive build-up of troops for Operation Overlord got well under way.

SATURDAY 5th

The Wentworth's are having some more American officers to stay tomorrow and I am doing the cooking again – I am being very generously rewarded I must say, so no complaints, especially as Monty is so welcome there. I am giving them game pie as there are so many pheasants and pigeons about.

March 1944

On March 9th the Daily Express headline read '1,000 Forts, 2,000 Tons – and only 38 Lost'; this referred to one of the largest American daylight raids of the war, on Berlin: again, to quote the Express '1,000 bombs fell for each square mile of the city'. The ordnance carried by the Fortresses and Liberators comprised 500 and 1,000 pounders. The effect on German morale can be imagined. The war was entering the endgame: during this time the British had not been idle as Bomber Command commenced its preparations in northern France for D-Day.

In Norfolk there was a pervasive atmosphere of anticipation, of the end now 'hoving' into view – Betty had her doubts.

TUESDAY 14th

Had a day working in the garden. I cannot say that I have gone short, or most of the people I know. What with Fred and his gun, Jack and him being such good gardeners who have shown anyone who didn't know how to, to grow vegetables. And not to forget young Freddie and his 'ways and means'. I know from friends, who live in cities, that there it has not been so easy. My garden has kept me in most vegetables, apart from potatoes which take up to much ground. And not to forget the chickens and ducks who have more than done their bit on the home front.

WEDNESDAY 29th

Abe, George and Randolph came round this afternoon to say goodbye. They have all finished their tour and are going home to America. Randolph said that the first thing he will do when he gets home is to get a dog like Monty. He has really taken to him and when he comes in the pub spends more time talking to him than to anyone else. There they sit with Monty holding his head this way and that listening to every word. It will be sad to see them go but good that they are, as so many of their mates will not be. It is hard to think how many of the young faces we have lost in the past four years and it is not over yet by a long chalk. Mr. Wentworth told me once that the last part of the war would be the most difficult. He is away in Bushy at the moment. Mrs. Wentworth says she will not see much of him for the next few months, what with the planning of the invasion and all that.

WAR BONDS WERE BOUGHT TO SUPPORT THE ARMED FORCES

April 1944

The war ground on in all theatres: in Japan the allied forces made inevitable progress against the Japanese; the Russians reached Romania; 230,000 German troops were withdrawn from the Crimea and the RAF continued to prepare the ground for D-Day with some of the heaviest bombing so far on northern France. The famous Mosquito raid on Gestapo HQ in The Hague entered the annals of remarkable feats of warfare.

THURSDAY 6th

Beryl showed me her book where she keeps the names of all the airmen that have been in the pub since the start of the war. Not all of course but most. It was so sad to see all those names and to think how many of them have given their lives in the last five years.

FRIDAY 7th (GOOD FRIDAY)

Mr. Head came into Doris's today to tell me that he had decided to take up the offer of going to stay with his relatives for a fortnight to see if he liked it. I said that he had nothing to lose and that if he did like it, it would be a nice change for him to have family around him, and that he would be better off not having to pay all his bills and rent. I know that part of the world and it is lovely in the summer. I have spent many a long summer day walking the beaches in Eastbourne, Bournemouth and Brighton and most of the places in between. When the war is over all those places will soon get back to normal and that's a fact. I always got on well with the people down there in the digs and in the theatres.

SUNDAY 30th

Monty and I went for a very long walk this morning. Monty had a rare old time sniffling about in the bushes in Bluebell Wood. The smell of Spring is one of the things I shall remember most about Norfolk should I ever move on. Jennifer has lined herself up with a place to train as a nurse after the war, so what with Mr. Head leaving things look as though they will not be the same. Stanley has said he is thinking of what he will do too.

May 1944

In the wider world allied progress continued: what was left of the Germans in the Crimea was crushed and Cassino fell to the British.

This was the month when the most important decision of the war was made: the date of the allied invasion of Europe. As the greatest invasion force the world has ever seen gathered in the south of England, Eisenhower decided, according to some sources, to make that decision on May 8th. From that point the die was cast – and the Rubicon well and truly crossed. 47 RAF officers were shot while escaping from Stalag III; this was the incident that inspired the film 'The Great Escape' and was one of the most heinous acts of murder in the annals of war.

On the European mainland a massive 5,000-bomber raid was carried out upon 12 railways and nine airfields in Belgium and France.

For the first time in three years the casualty count in Britain was zero.

FRIDAY 12th

Mrs. Wentworth has been staying with friends near Gravesend and visited one of the local hospitals. The roads down south are full of army traffic and Mrs. Wentworth thinks that the invasion is not far off now.

MONDAY 15th

Mr. Head has had a letter from his relations telling him that everything was ready for him when he wanted to visit.

June 1944

This was the BBC Home Service broadcast: "Early this morning the allies began the assault on the north western face of Hitler's Fortress Europe. And here is a special bulletin read by John Snagge. D-Day has come..." With those words, just after 9.30 in the morning, the people of Britain were informed of the start of the largest invasion in history: Operation Overlord. The statistics are, even by today's standards, staggering – the force raged against the Nazis comprised 11,500 aircraft – a third of which were bombers whose job was to destroy as much of the German's ability to defend themselves as possible; the thousands of allied fighters were to demonstrate, in as potent a way as could have been wished, the benefit of air superiority. Then there were the ships. An awesome armada of 4,000. One eyewitness told of ships "filling the horizon". War, however, is an uncertain business: In General Eisenhower's wallet, at the start of Overlord, was a press release. This is what it said: "Our landings in the Cherbourg-Havre area have failed to gain a satisfactory foothold and I have withdrawn the troops. My decision to attack at this time and place was based upon the best information available. The troops, the air and the Navy did all that bravery and devotion to duty could do. If any blame or fault attaches to the attempt it is mine and mine alone." That press release was, mercifully, not needed.

In Norfolk Betty, understandably, spent little time writing in her diary. But what she did say gives a flavour of the jubilation in the air.

MONTGOMERY, EISENHOWER AND OTHERS IN THE FIELD

TUESDAY 6th (D-DAY)

Just the news we were all waiting for. Stanley was so pleased, I have not seen him so happy for ages. I was helping out at the pub this morning and Fred, George and Ted were giving Monty Guinness. They said that as Montgomery is not likely to drop in for a drink they would buy one for his namesake.

Mrs. Wentworth came in and invited us to a party on Friday to celebrate the good news.

George opened the back room tonight and we had a good drink or two with our supper and listened to the King at nine o'clock. Young Freddie brought me some pig's trotters the day before yesterday and I had made six one pound brawns. They went down very well with some of Beryl's chutney and my bread. Jack said that from now on pork brawn would always remind him of today.

FRIDAY 9th

Had a lovely time at Mrs. Wentworth's. Her Uncle Peverell is staying there for a week or two. What a character he is. Six feet six and a back as straight as a ramrod. He is a veteran of the Sudan and is full of stories. He said that now we are back in France it won't be very long before we start "organising some manners in those damned Nazis".

July 1944

In Normandy the allies advanced on Caen. Montgomery pushed forward through the enemy's holding line around the Normandy bridgehead; an awesome tank battle lasted for days. Monty wrote a personal letter of thanks to Arthur 'Bomber' Harris for the work of Bomber Command during the invasion. The Germans launched nine attacks, each failing to halt the ally's progress. In the South of England the V1 terror had begun. The headlines in the Evening News said it all: 'Flying bombs kill 2,752, injure 8,000: Very high toll in London'. V1s rained down at the rate of 150 a day, with a death rate of one death per bomb.

On July 21st Hitler made a broadcast to tell the German people of a failed attempt to assassinate him; in the aftermath the Furher exacted a cruel revenge on the perpetrators – including Colonel Graf von Stauffenberg. One can only guess at what would have happened had the plot succeeded.

UNDATED

Just when we are hearing about the job our boys are doing in Normandy these flying bombs start dropping. Mrs. Wentworth's friend Caroline Stowe was only a few yards from where one blew up a row of houses. She caught some of the blast and has had to have stitches but is alright. Mr. Head is off down to Eastbourne for a month to see how he likes it. I think he has made up his mind to move though.

THE PREPARATION OF
A **VI FLYING BOMB**
OTHERWISE KNOWN
AS A 'DOODLEBUG'

THURSDAY 13th

In the Daily Sketch today it says how Rommel is abandoning his wounded as he is running so fast. What a right old lot those Germans are, and even Rommel.

August 1944

In Normandy the bloody battle for Caen raged – a vital objective of the invasion was to proceed as planned. Those involved in the plot to assassinate Hitler came to a sticky end. Churchill payed a visit to Normandy and had face-to-face briefings, on the progress of the invasion, from Montgomery and General Bradley. In the middle of the month Allied forces landed on the southern coast of France and the bombardment of Berlin continued. The breaking of the morale of Germany was no less important at this stage of the war than earlier.

In Norfolk news of the Nazis terror weapons was causing concern.

KEEP VIGILANT

WEDNESDAY 16th

I had a couple of hours at Mrs. Wentworth's this morning. She told me about how strange it is for her to read of the battle that is raging in France because when she was a girl she spent many happy days near Falaise. Her aunt lived there and she and her cousin used to stay in the summer. I told her that one day she will be able to go back, after all Churchill is there now.

THE **V2 FLYING BOMB**. THE TECHNOLOGY WAS REVOLUTIONARY

SATURDAY 26th

There is a worrying little story in the Daily Mail about another sort of flying bomb, this time called the V2. I wonder what it will do. I just hope they don't start sending them up here. Beryl had a letter from a friend whose husband is in the fire brigade in London and she says that the last few weeks have been a nightmare.

September 1944

The headline in the News Chronicle for Friday 1st said it all: '400,000 German casualties, including 47 divisions destroyed, mauled or trapped; in material the enemy has lost 1,300 tanks, 2,000 guns, and 3,500 planes.'

General Montgomery, said by Eisenhower to be "one of the great soldiers of this or any war", was promoted to Field Marshal – a decision that found few, if any, critics – at least not on the allied side; the buzz-bomb menace continued, in the week ending September 5th some 370 fell on southern England – making a total of around 8,100 since the attacks began. In Germany the Gestapo began a reign of terror against the civil population – a desperate reaction to approaching defeat.

In Norfolk the other good news was much appreciated.

THURSDAY 7th

After all this time, it seems like a lifetime but of course it isn't, the blackout will soon be over (from the 17th) and the call-up to the Home Guard is being stopped. I don't know what that will mean for Jack and the boys. Will they wind them up? I know they all like to feel they are doing their bit, but those cold old winter guard duties don't do any of them any good.

WEDNESDAY 20th

I was early at the pub this morning and that is where I heard the news about our boys reaching the Rhine. George said that he thinks Montgomery's tail is well up now that he is a Field Marshal. There were a few of the boys from Swanton Morley in and we all had a drink at lunchtime, some more than was good for them.

FRIDAY 22nd

Mavis is full of it today. The plans for demobbing have been in the paper. There was a bit of a nip in the air tonight as I walked home from the pub with Monty. He doesn't feel the cold him being what Harry calls 'a tough little highlander'. I can't remember what it was like before I had young Monty. I had a letter from Mr. Head and he says he is having a good time, is being well looked after and is being made to feel like one of the family. He said that he is thinking of getting a dog, as he misses Monty, and did I think Harry would be able to get one for him.

October 1944

Forward area troops on the mainland of Europe, who were the cutting edge of the D-Day invasion, were granted the dubious privilege of 'leave', the only drawback being that they had to spend it 'over there', billeted at 'quiet hotels and guest houses' in Brussels. The plan was that the men should have forty-eight hours leave every six months. Elsewhere in France and Belgium Montgomery steadily tightened the screw on the enemy; in what appeared an act of desperation the Germans used the V1 for the first time as a front line weapon on the American First Army. In the south east of England the doodlebugs continued to rain down.

Summer gently changed to autumn and Betty and her friends were as industrious as ever – and Monty heard of a visit from a relative.

TUESDAY 10th

I was saying to Mrs. Wentworth this morning how much we have learned since the start of the war. I can remember how most people around here were worried that we might go short of food. But we have, on the whole, been quite well provided for, one way and another. Mrs. Wentworth says as how our government were wise in the way they handled rationing, not rationing bread and such like, but that in the cities it has not been so easy, what with them not having the benefits and fruits of the country-side. I think folk like Fred, young Freddie and Jack should get medals for the way they have provided and put food on all our tables. I have learned a lot about gardening and preserving what we grow.

TUESDAY 31st

Harry turned up today out of the blue with Mr. Head's little dog, Ruby, a sister of Monty. I wrote and told him Mr. Head would be coming to stay for a few days and that it would be a good idea if he stayed as well so he could make sure Mr. Head knew all the things he had to do to keep the little pup happy and well. She is a lovely little thing with coal black eyes and legs like little tree stumps. Jack said she is as well made as Monty. Monty is as good as ever and leading Ruby all over the place showing her around. Mr. Head gets here tomorrow at about eleven. His rooms are ready and it will be nice to see him again.

November 1944

Once again the newspaper headlines told the story very well, the taking of the first big German town: 'AACHEN FALLS'; 'ALL BELGIUM IS FREE'; and referring to the massive allied offensive from Holland to the Alps 'EISENHOWER LAUNCHES HIS KNOCK-OUT BLOW'; and the most evocative of them all 'BRITISH BITE INTO THE SIEGFRIED BACKBONE'.

Some of the many strangers to these shores were going home.

FRIDAY 17th

Mr. Head and Ruby are getting on well, Harry is going home on Friday and he says that Ruby is in good hands. Monty, Polly and Starter have spent the afternoon playing in Bluebell Wood with Harry. They were in a right old state when they came in and needed a good going over with a towel, and me in the middle of the weekend baking for the shop.

SATURDAY 18th

Harry says I should think about getting a friend for Monty. I wonder just how many pups he can lay his hands on at the rate he is going.

December 1944

It was that time of year again and Betty was, as expected, preparing for the festivities. There was a feeling in the air of an end to hostilities not being far away but nobody was feeling over-confident for fear of tempting fate. The casualty lists continued to grow as the V2 menace continued to take a terrible toll in the south, 716 in November alone, an increase on October. In Holland Spitfire bombers attacked marshalling yards where the deadly rockets were loaded. In the Ardennes the Battle of the Bulge was raging as Von Runstedt made his final move.

Betty's Christmas got under way.

THURSDAY 21st

Spent the day at the pub washing the big pans ready for Christmas. It will be funny Mr. Head not being here this year. He wrote to me today and said that Ruby is settling in well. She is a good companion and sees that he has his exercise what with walking her and the like. Jennifer told Mavis that she thinks she will be going back to Manchester in the New Year. She will be missed, but the war will not last long now and she is keen to start nursing again as soon as she can.

FRIDAY 22nd

Mavis and Jennifer have been decorating the room at the pub ready for Christmas Eve. Jennifer has an eye for that sort of thing, she would be good in the theatre, she really would. Alfred's painting of Father Christmas and his reindeer is hanging along the big wall and the tree is to the far end. A big one provided by Fred and a lovely shape. Mrs. Wentworth gave me some glass decorations that she has had for years but has never used as she has so many family pieces she has collected over the years. She says they are like old friends.

CHRISTMAS EVE

We had a rare old time tonight at the pub, lots of Christmas spirit in more ways than one. Monty and Albert were a picture walking about together getting made a fuss of. Young Freddie put in an appearance to give me some biscuits for Monty, and Ted and Jack were playing darts for whisky. Jack will have a head on him tomorrow. George and Beryl have an Uncle Harold staying, an old navy man who holds forth with stories of all the battles he has been in. A real old salt, beard and all, and one for the rum too.

HAPPY CHRISTMAS 1944

DAY AFTER BOXING DAY

A lovely Christmas day. Twelve of us for dinner and what a meal it was. As George said it is one to remember. The goose Jack provided was so tasty and Beryl must take all the credit for it being so good. As it was so good we had three of Fred's pheasants left over and we had them cold today with pickles, baked potatoes and chutney. Monty and Albert had a good fill and slept until gone seven o'clock. After Christmas dinner we opened the presents. Mrs. Wentworth sent us round a case of wine with a note wishing us all a Merry Christmas and inviting me to have a drink with her and some friends on New Year. Hard to credit that it will be 1945 so soon.

New Year 1944/45

While the two opposing armies battled to the death on mainland Europe thoughts began to turn to home affairs: the Daily Express, January 16th, revealed on its front page a new service to its readers, the General Election Bureau. The main purpose of which was to collate information about constituencies and the new candidates – it was expected that some 400 sitting MPs would be standing down before the next polling day. One way or another the country was in for some big changes, changes that were to affect the lives of all for the rest of the century.

In Norfolk Betty celebrated the New Year in style.

NEW YEARS EVE

George has taken the beer over to Mrs. Wentworth's already and Mavis has been busy doing the last minute baking. I went with Jack this afternoon to take the birds and my pickles and chutney. It looks like being a good party. It is a shame young Freddie won't be here as he is staying with his aunt.

NEW YEARS DAY

Mrs. Wentworth really did us all proud last night. It is the first time since 1939 that she has opened up her big room. She had put up trestle tables in three rows and each was set out like a West End hotel, it really was. She had Charlie in to move the wireless so that we had some music and the BBC did their bit in giving us some good tunes for the occasion. George and Beryl did not manage to get there until late but Mavis, Jack, Fred, Ted, Jennifer, her friend Elaine, Stanley and some friends of Mrs. Wentworth all arrived at about seven. Stanley had made a great big banner that said 'Peace This Year' with a picture of Hitler behind bars in the corner. I don't think it was tempting fate to say that. This spring will see an end to it. We had a good spread to eat. Doris said it was one of her best orders for years. Pork pies, mince pies, two Christmas cakes I made using fruit and flour from Mrs. Wentworth's friends who are staying, cold pheasant, chicken and lots of different pickles and chutneys that everyone contributed. We all had a good time eating drinking and talking. Later Fred took us all outside for a surprise. He has been putting a chestnut engine together that he found in an old shed he was clearing out for someone. I have not seen one for years and years. It is like a little train with a fire in the bottom and a grill to roast the chestnuts. We had a lovely time peeling and eating, with Fred playing the Hot Chestnut Man. It took me back years. By the time we had finished it was 1945.

Jack, George, Beryl, Mavis and I stayed later than the others to help clear away, even though Mrs. Wentworth said we shouldn't. We stayed until gone three o'clock. It was one of the best New Year's for a long time and the last of this war I am sure.

February 1945

This was the month that saw the 'Big Three' meeting at Yalta. The results of these talks would reverberate until the end of the century. The final communiqué from the talks elicited a not unexpected response from Paul Schmidt, German Foreign Office spokesman. In short he said "The Yalta declaration released Germany from all moral scruples. Every enemy, no matter when or how he penetrates into Germany, will be met by fanatical men, women and children, who know what treatment is in store for them and therefore wish to kill, murder and poison all who attempt to oppress them." With these words, published with the permission of the German Foreign Office, Germany's descent into the lowest depths of depravity was complete. The end, when it came, would be bloody and defeat complete.

In Norfolk Betty visited a 'good Samaritan'.

WEDNESDAY 14th

The boys from Shipdham are pleased as punch with the latest raids on Germany and really rolled out the barrel. Max said as how he felt they were dishing it out to the 'Krauts' like they deserve and Dresden was only the start.

THURSDAY 15th

We were talking in the pub tonight about the talks at Yalta. George says it shows just what Jerry is in for soon. Jack says that it would be a good thing to take Germany off the map altogether for what they have done. He thinks all of Germany should be given to Holland.

SATURDAY 17th

Fred came round this morning and told me to come and see what he had found. In his big shed he had a young fox, a vixen, not yet a year old he thinks. He found her by the side of the road unconscious near Bluebell Wood and with her front leg all twisted. Fred took her home and found that she had a badly broken leg. He managed to set and splint it before she came round. He did it with wood, linen and wire. When I saw her she was up and about but looking a bit sad and sleepy. Monty gave her a good old sniff through the wire of the cage. Fred told me that if he had not been quick he would never have been able to splint her up. He did a good job by the look of it, the leg looks nice and straight. Fred is not new to foxes as he had one called Fergus when he was a boy. He asked me not to say anything to strangers, as some people don't like our red-haired cousins. He calls her Bluebell.

March 1945

The news from the former 'Fortress Europe' was encouraging: armour of the American First Army broke through ten miles from Cologne. Elsewhere, in a move that sent a pulse of terror through the Germans, the Russians drove towards Berlin. One headline said it all: 'NO OPPOSITION NOW TO OUR DRIVE – MONTY'S TANKS RUN WILD IN EUROPE'.

April 1945

On mainland Europe the enemy was being soundly defeated. Eisenhower partially lifted the security blackout in order to let the good news out that the allies were 100 miles beyond the Rhine. In so many places the British and American forces thrust the dagger of the endgame deep into the Nazi heart. In the 4,800 square mile pocket of the Ruhr 50,000 Germans faced death or surrender. Across the middle of Germany – on April 2nd – General Patton's armour powered towards the Czech frontier and was only 165 miles from Berlin; by the 12th the distance had closed to 64 miles.

On April 13th President Roosevelt, one of the staunchest of our allies, died. In a White House statement it was said "He did his job to the end, as he would want to". Harry Truman took the reigns.

As the Germans withdrew from Holland the V weapon menace evaporated. As an indication of how things were going Paris turned on its lights for the first time since the outbreak of war.

As the month drew to a close the Russians reached Berlin and exacted a terrible revenge on their most hated of enemies.

At 4.20pm on the 25th the Americans and Russians met up at Torgau on the River Elbe – effectively cutting Germany in half.

In Norfolk a wanderer returned.

MONDAY 2nd (EASTER MONDAY)

Mr. Head is settled in at the pub with Ruby. She has grown into a sturdy little dog, just like Monty. He arrived just in time for Good Friday. So I gave him his hot cross buns like in the old days. It has been quite a quiet Easter weekend. We have been listening to all the news we can on the wireless as things are moving fast now. Mrs. Wentworth told me that it would be over in Europe in a month. Mr. Head says that he is staying here until it is over now, to see it finish where he saw it start.

What news, Mussolini has been hanged, and not before time. Let's hope it's not long before the same thing happens to Hitler. This war has made us all capable of thinking terrible things, but those Germans are to blame and I don't suppose any of us will ever be the same as we were.

May 1945

This was an important month, not just by local standards but also in the history of the world. On the first day of May it was obvious that the war in Europe was all but won. Nazi broadcasts on Hamburg radio – the only station left standing – endeavoured to prepare a defeated German population for occupation by Allied forces.

Then, on May 2nd, the headlines proclaimed the death of the most evil monster the world has ever produced: 'HITLER IS DEAD'. With those three words the long fought for victory was rubber-stamped. Later, on Luneburg Heath Admiral Donetz surrendered to Montgomery.

In Norfolk the celebrations were fitting.

**VE DAY
CELEBRATIONS**
MAY 8TH 1945

WEDNESDAY 2nd

At last, Hitler has got his comeuppance. We have had such a day in the pub as I can hardly believe. Not a glum face or a cross word. After so long we are there. The war will soon be over and the boys really will be coming home, not to go away again we pray. Mrs. Wentworth came by to see me and said she was having some friends in to celebrate. I am going there tomorrow evening with Mavis and Jennifer if she is not working. It seems so peculiar to see the headlines 'HITLER IS DEAD'. George has pinned it up over the bar and all night some of us have just looked at it and looked at it. Monty was given far too much Guinness tonight and he could hardly walk home. He fell asleep as soon as he got in. I hope he is not getting into bad habits, the little mite.

MONDAY 7th

Fred, Monty and I went to the woods today to see Bluebell. She is better now and you would never guess that she had had a broken leg. Fred called her and she came. Not too close, but just enough so we could see her. He is a kind man Fred.

VE DAY

Two days holiday and what a time we have had. All of us have felt so happy that we are there at last. All those black days, Dunkirk, the fall of France and the Low Countries. One day I shall read what I wrote back then, but not for a long time. This is a time to look forward and not back. Jennifer is leaving soon to go to train to be a nurse, she will be missed. But so many of our friends will now be coming home and we may be able to get back to normal. Mrs. Wentworth was saying that it may take a bit before we are off the rations but it won't seem anything like as bad.

June 1945

The war entered its final stages following Hitler's death.

SATURDAY 14th

Fred has been doing some gardening for the vicar. His garden was in a right old state, Fred was quite annoyed as, like he said, for the last few years we have all been growing as much food as we can for ourselves and others and here is this huge garden just lying idle. Not very patriotic and I shall tell the vicar when I see him. All very well getting up every Sunday and preaching but like Fred says "it's not what you say, it's what you do, that wins wars", and he's right.

SATURDAY 21st

Mavis and Jennifer have had a 'day on the beach' in the pub garden. They are a pair. There they were in their deckchairs listening to the wireless on the windowsill. It was a lovely day.

July 1945

FRIDAY 27th

Nice surprises today as some old faces turned up at the pub. We had a drink to them and another to all the lads still fighting the Japanese.

August 1945

THE DAY THAT SHOOK THE WORLD

In Europe peace was breaking out as much as it could. Day to day life carried on much as before, but the shadow of war was lifting. The American presence was diminishing, leaving some bad feeling behind them over the destruction of stores which, some thought, could have been put to better use – hardly a surprising reaction among a population to whom the humble banana was little more than legend.

On August 6th the American Bomber, Enola Gay, dropped the first atomic bomb to be used in anger upon Hiroshima. The devastation caused surprised everyone; the scale of the destruction their baby had wrought took even those who devised the weapon aback. The shadow of the Atomic Age was about to fall upon an unsuspecting world. It is no exaggeration to say that the world would never be the same again.

Following the dropping of the second A-bomb on Nagasaki, Japan's surrender was inevitable and the allies shed few tears. Japan gave up the fight on August 15th.

WEDNESDAY 8th

I don't understand about this new bomb at all. Mrs. Wentworth tried to explain but it is beyond me. All I can see is that one bomb dropped on the Japanese has destroyed a city. How can that be? I mean, in the Blitz they dropped hundreds and hundreds and we still carried on. So how can one bomb do all what it says in the papers? Jack said that it was only a bomber like around here so it can't have been a very big bomb.

OPPOSITE: **THE INSTRUMENT OF SURRENDER** ISSUED ON
BEHALF OF THE EMPEROR OF JAPAN, THE JAPANESE GOVERNMENT
AND THE JAPANESE IMPERIAL GENERAL HEADQUARTERS

INSTRUMENT OF SURRENDER

e, acting by command of and in behalf of the Emperor of Japan, the Japanese Government and the Japanese Imperial General Headquarters, hereby accept the provisions set forth in the declaration issued by the heads of the Governments of the United States, China and Great Britain on 26 July 1945, at Potsdam, and subsequently adhered to by the Union of Soviet Socialist Republics, which four powers are hereafter referred to as the Allied Powers.

We hereby proclaim the unconditional surrender to the Allied Powers of the Japanese Imperial General Headquarters and of all Japanese armed forces and all armed forces under Japanese control wherever situated.

We hereby command all Japanese forces wherever situated and the Japanese people to cease hostilities forthwith, to preserve and save from damage all ships, aircraft, and military and civil property and to comply with all requirements which may be imposed by the Supreme Commander for the Allied Powers or by agencies of the Japanese Government at his direction.

We hereby command the Japanese Imperial General Headquarters to issue at once orders to the Commanders of all Japanese forces and all forces under Japanese control wherever situated to surrender unconditionally themselves and all forces under their control.

We hereby command all civil, military and naval officials to obey and enforce all proclamations, orders and directives deemed by the Supreme Commander for the Allied Powers to be proper to effectuate this surrender and issued by him or under his authority and we direct all such officials to remain at their posts and to continue to perform their non-combatant duties unless specifically relieved by him or under his authority.

We hereby undertake for the Emperor, the Japanese Government and their successors to carry out the provisions of the Potsdam Declaration in good faith, and to issue whatever orders and take whatever action may be required by the Supreme Commander for the Allied Powers or by any other designated representative of the Allied Powers for the purpose of giving effect to that Declaration.

We hereby command the Japanese Imperial Government and the Japanese Imperial General Headquarters at once to liberate all allied prisoners of war and civilian internees now under Japanese control and to provide for their protection, care, maintenance and immediate transportation to places as directed.

The authority of the Emperor and the Japanese Government to rule the state shall be subject to the Supreme Commander for the Allied Powers who will take such steps as he deems proper to effectuate these terms of surrender.

September 1945

Four most waited and prayed for words: 'The War is over'. The most barbaric conflict civilisation had ever seen had, after six long years, come to an end. With the surrender of Japan, following the dropping of the first two atomic bombs on Hiroshima and Nagasaki, peace came in the Far East as well as Europe. Many challenges were ahead, and the privations of war would extend into the post-war period. However, the shadow of war was all that was left, the conflict proper was over.

In Norfolk Betty and her friends decided to have a knees-up.

UNDATED

George has been sorting out things for the party. It will only be for close friends and acquaintances as he has had trouble before for serving after hours so he wants to be careful. Freddie has given me a case of whisky, where on earth he got it I don't know, but he told me he had been saving it for the end of the war and this is it, so he wants to share it round. I took a bottle up to Mr. Head's room and hid it under his pillow as a surprise while he was out walking with Ruby.

Jack and Stanley are helping Beryl with the food. I am just too busy baking for Doris. Orders are well up and the money is very handy, I can tell you. One thing this war hasn't done is made any of us rich, bar a few I can mention who I hope will feel guilty about how they have behaved these past years, most of them butchers I have to say. Mrs. Wentworth says she is going to boycott all the tradesmen that were badly behaved and I am sure she will. I asked her to come to the party at the pub and she said she would not miss it for all the tea in China. Looks like we shall have a full turnout to see the war out and peace in.

THE PARTY OF ALL PARTIES

I have a terrible headache. I can't remember how much I must have had to drink. I think I must have mixed things too much. I remember George finding Ted in the cellar and thought he had fallen down the steps and knocked himself out, but he had just passed out from a bottle of London Gin Freddie had given him. He was still there when I went to bed at four o'clock. I put his jacket under his head and left him. My goodness there was some drink shifted last night. I have been to some booze-ups in my time but that was the best. Edgar (the local Bobby) warned George about serving after hours, and that when he came he would come round the back out of uniform and knock four times, as he did not want to miss a drop himself. He turned up just after midnight and could hardly walk by two. Well, why shouldn't he have a drink, he was not really on duty.

Now, as Mrs. Wentworth said just after we listened to the nine o'clock news: "it is up to all of us to do what we can, to do justice to the bravery of the fallen by seeing that we make the most of the peace and freedom they have bequeathed us."

We all drank a toast to that.

"HE'S TAKEN A TURN

FOR THE NURSE"

A MUTOSCOPE CARD   PRINTED IN U. S. A.

List of illustrations

Index

A

C

S